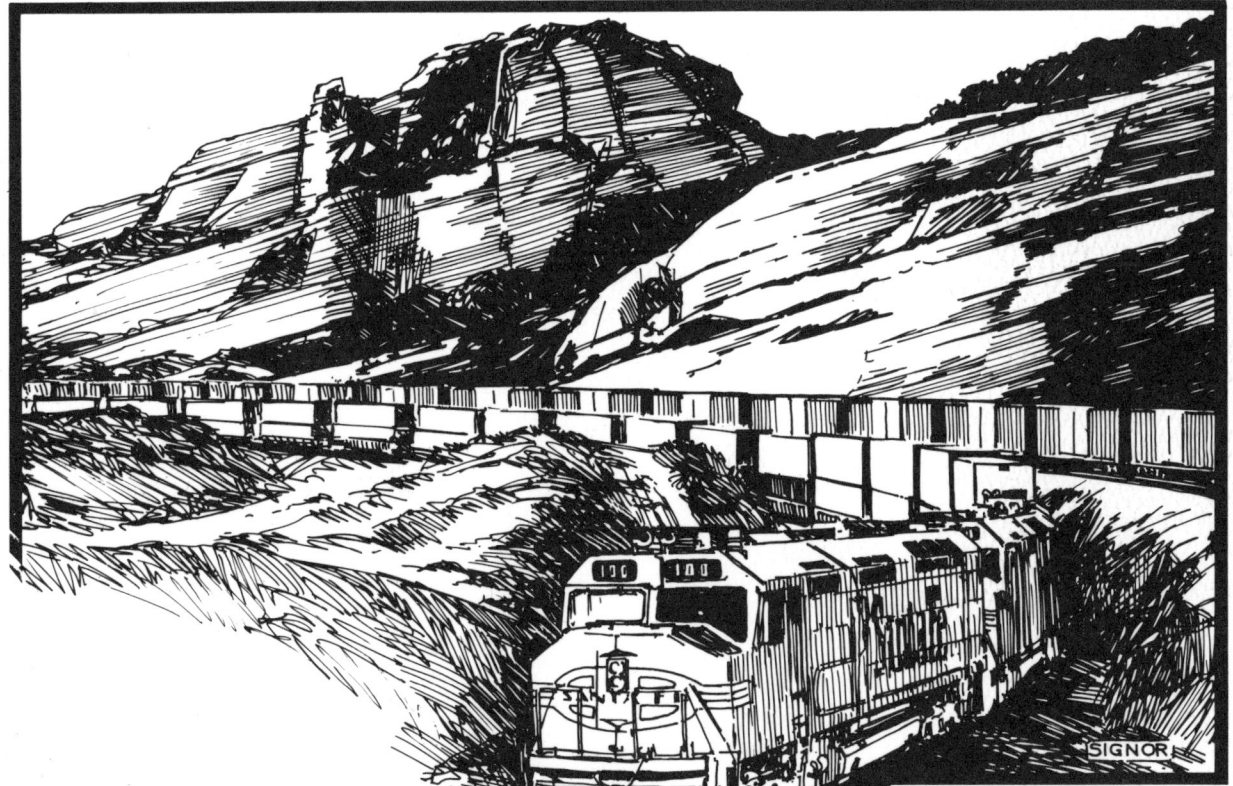

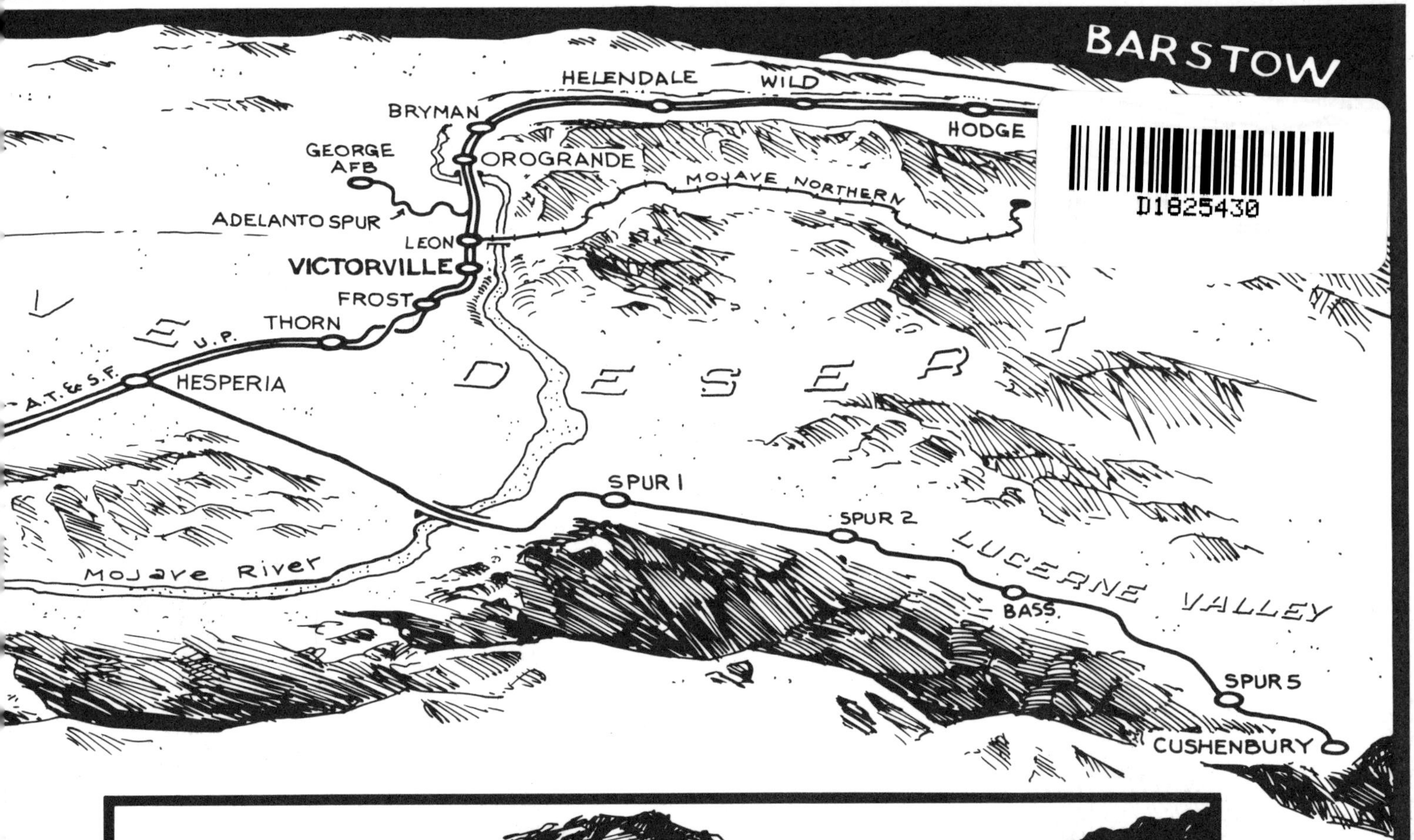
BARSTOW
HELENDALE
WILD
BRYMAN
HODGE
GEORGE AFB
OROGRANDE
MOJAVE NORTHERN
ADELANTO SPUR
LEON
VICTORVILLE
FROST
THORN
U.P.
A.T.&S.F.
HESPERIA
DESERT
SPUR 1
SPUR 2
Mojave River
LUCERNE VALLEY
BASS
SPUR 5
CUSHENBURY
AND
Ana Wash

SIGNOR

CAJON PASS

Chard Walker's

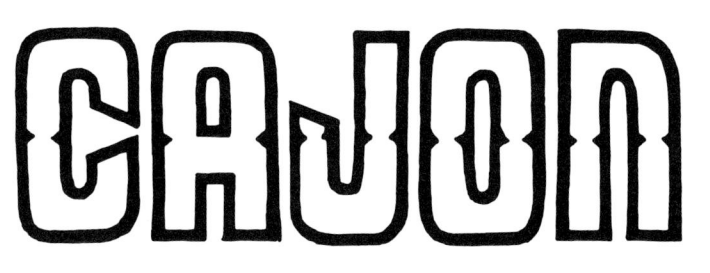

A Pictorial Album

Chard Walker's

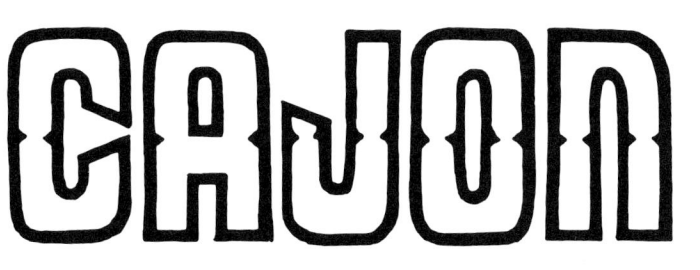

A Pictorial Album

San Bernardino to Victorville

Trans-Anglo Books
Glendale, California

Cover: With a quartet of red and silver ''Super Fleet'' FP45s in charge, Santa Fe Extra 105 East storms up the approach to Sullivan's Curve, just east of Cajon Station on January 6, 1990.
Elrond G. Lawrence

Rear Cover Top: UP E9A 905 leads westbound train No. 9 through the ''big curve'' west of Summit on January 6, 1957. *Allan Styffe*

Rear Cover Center: Seen from the cab of UP helper unit 1619 (an Alco FA), Santa Fe First 7, the first section of the westbound Fast Mail Express, rapidly approaches with EMD FT unit 163 on the point. The location is just west of Hesperia on this May 12, 1949 day. *Chard L. Walker*

Rear Cover Bottom: The Lucerne Valley Range forms a snow-covered backdrop as Southern Pacific 8969 West rolls through Hesperia, passing under Interstate 15 on its way to Palmdale on a sunny March 21, 1982. *Chard L. Walker*

© 1990 by Chard L. Walker

Manufactured in the United States of America

First Printing: Spring 1990

Published by
TRANS-ANGLO BOOKS
a division of
Interurban Press
P.O. Box 6444 Glendale, California 91225

Library of Congress Cataloguing-in-Publication Data

Walker, Chard L.
    Cajon, a pictorial album : San Bernardino to Victorville /
by Chard Walker.
      p. cm.
    ISBN 0-87046-095-1
    1. Railroads—California—Cajon Pass—Pictorial works.
2. Cajon Pass (Calif.)—Description and travel—Views. I. Title.
TF24.C3W34 1990
385'.09794'95—dc20   90-34707
                                    CIP
                                      AC

Book Design, Layout and Production
James W. Reese
Elrond G. Lawrence

Color Separations
Jim Walter Graphics
Beloit, Wisconsin

Typesetting
Roc-Pacific
Los Angeles, California

DEDICATION

To my grandchildren, Sarah and Jessica Hover, and
Andrew and Kimberly Jacobson, so that someday they can
learn of the era that "Paw" experienced

PREFACE

While preparing *Cajon—Rail Passage to the Pacific,* the author amassed a huge number of photos from his many railfan friends. Unfortunately, only a fraction of the photos on hand could be included in the book due to space limitations. The purpose of this volume is to share some of the photos that were not included in the earlier book as well as updating the material with all-new photography.

The publisher has suggested that a larger selection of color photos be included in this volume, and the author feels that everyone who sees this album will agree that it was a mighty fine suggestion. The photos included in both the color and in the black and white sections have been arranged in geographical order, starting at San Bernardino

and continuing up the grade to Summit, then downgrade to Victorville. Photos of the Southern Pacific line constructed in 1967 will be found in the appropriate locations adjacent to the Santa Fe line (over which Union Pacific and Amtrak operate via trackage rights).

It should be kept in mind that timetable directions on the SP are westward when headed toward San Francisco and eastward when headed away from there. So in the Cajon Pass area where SP and AT&SF lines more or less parallel each other between Dike/Devore and Hiland/Summit, trains ascending the grade on the SP are westbound while those on the AT&SF are eastbound, and vice versa.

On November 16, 1985, photographer Leon Callaway discovered this truck parked near the Santa Fe tracks at Cajon station. The author's date of November 9, 1885, refers to when the final spike was driven, while Mike Martin of Santa Fe's Public Relations Department refers to when regular service began on November 16, 1885. The rock formations in the center of the photo are close to Sullivan's Curve. *Leon Callaway*

TABLE OF CONTENTS

ACKNOWLEDGEMENTS

Without the generous contributions of photos from the photographers and collectors listed below (in alphabetical order), this album would not have been possible. To these people the author extends his thanks and appreciation. In addition, he wishes to thank Mike Martin of the Santa Fe for the 1989 timetable, and Marty Banks and Richard Weigle for the track warrants and track bulletins and general information. If the author has overlooked any contributor, he apologizes. Any such oversights were unintentional.

James Ady
Arthur Anderson
Ray Ballash
Henry Brueckman
David Busse
Leon Callaway
C. H. Clevenger
Harold Dague
George Drury (*Trains* magazine)
Bill Farmer
Bob Finan
Malcolm Gaddis
Gordon Glattenberg
The late Jeff Goodwill
Bob Gottier
Hank Graham
Robert Hale
Lewis Harris
Robert Heuerman
Rod Higbie
The late Thomas Hotchkiss
The late Freeman Hubbard
   (*Railroad* magazine)
Fred Hust
Randy Keller
Bob Kern
Richard Kindig

Stan Kistler
Elrond Lawrence
Mike Lepker
David Longshore
Alex Mayes
C. W. McLaughlin
Joe McMillan
The late Robert McVay
Ralph Melching
Alan Miller
Jim Minor
Martin Orozco
Alton Parsons
Steve Patterson
Santa Fe Railway
John Shaw
Donald Sims
John Sistrunk
Steele's Photo Service
Richard Steinheimer
Dick Stephenson
Alan Styffe
David Styffe
Fletcher Swan
Union Pacific Railroad
Jack Whitmeyer
Allan Youell

TRACK WARRANT

NO._____ _____19____
TO:_____ AT:_____

1. ☐ TRACK WARRANT NO. _____IS VOID.
2. ☐ PROCEED FROM _____
   TO _____ ON _____ TRACK.
3. ☐ PROCEED FROM _____
   TO _____ ON _____ TRACK.
4. ☐ WORK BETWEEN _____
   AND_____ON _____ TRACK.
5. ☐ NOT IN EFFECT UNTIL _____ M.
6. ☐ THIS AUTHORITY EXPIRES AT _____ M.
7. ☐ NOT IN EFFECT UNTIL AFTER ARRIVAL OF _____
   _____ AT _____ .
8. ☐ HOLD MAIN TRACK AT LAST NAMED POINT.
9. ☐ DO NOT FOUL LIMITS AHEAD OF_____.
10. ☐ CLEAR MAIN TRACK AT LAST NAMED POINT.
11. ☐ BETWEEN _____ AND _____ MAKE ALL MOVEMENTS AT RESTRICTED SPEED. LIMITS OCCUPIED BY TRAIN OR ENGINE.
12. ☐ BETWEEN _____ AND _____ MAKE ALL MOVEMENTS AT RESTRICTED SPEED AND STOP SHORT OF MEN OR MACHINES FOULING TRACK.
13. ☐ DO NOT EXCEED _____ MPH BETWEEN _____ AND _____ .
14. ☐ DO NOT EXCEED _____ MPH BETWEEN _____ AND _____ .
15. ☐ PROTECTION AS PRESCRIBED BY RULE 99 NOT REQUIRED.
16. ☐ TRACK BULLETINS IN EFFECT ____ , ____ , ____ , ____ , ____ , ____ , ____ , ____ , ____ , ____ , ____ , ____ , ____ , ____ , ____ .
17. ☐ OTHER SPECIFIC INSTRUCTIONS:_____
   _____
   _____
   _____

OK_____M DISPATCHER_____.
RELAYED TO_____COPIED BY_____.
LIMITS REPORTED CLEAR AT_____M BY_____.

(Mark ''X'' in box for each item instructed.)

FORM 1714 STD (REV. 10-85)

TRACK BULLETIN FORM B

NO. _____ ON _____ SUBDIV: _____ 19 _____
TO _____ AT _____
ON _____ BE GOVERNED BY RULE 455 WITHIN FOLLOWING LIMITS:
                    (DATE)
USE COLUMN WITH ASTERISK (*) WHEN FLAGS DISPLAYED LESS THAN DISTANCE PRESCRIBED BY RULE 10.

LINE VOID	LINE NO.	LIMITS MP TO MP	FROM	UNTIL	TRACK (S)	(*) FLAGS AT M.P.	FOREMAN AND GANG NO.	STOP
	1		M	M				
	2		M	M				
	3		M	M				
	4		M	M				
	5		M	M				
	6		M	M				
	7		M	M				
	8		M	M				
	9		M	M				
	10		M	M				

TOTAL LINES USED _____
OK _____ M COPIED BY _____ DISPATCHER _____
RELAYED TO _____

(FORM 1716 STD 9-85)

Chard Walker

TRACK BULLETIN FORM A

NO. _____ ON _____ SUBDIV. _____ 19 _____
TO _____ AT _____
BETWEEN POINTS SHOWN IN LINES 1 THROUGH 10 BELOW DO NOT EXCEED SPEED GIVEN; USE LAST COLUMN WHEN FLAGS DISPLAYED LESS THAN DISTANCE PRESCRIBED BY RULE 10.

LINE VOID	LINE NO	LIMITS MP TO MP	SPEED MPH	TRACK (S)	FLAGS AT M.P.
	1				
	2				
	3				
	4				
	5				
	6				
	7				
	8				
	9				
	10				
	11	OTHER CONDITIONS:			

TOTAL LINES USED _____
(FORM 1715 STD. 9-85) OK _____ M COPIED BY _____ DISPATCHER _____
RELAYED TO _____

Chard Walker

UPDATE

Several important changes have taken place on the railroads since *Cajon—Rail Passage to the Pacific* was published in 1985.

That same year, several railroads, including the Santa Fe, Southern Pacific and Union Pacific, adopted a new General Code of Operating Rules in which train orders, clearance cards, and even train order operators were eliminated. Instead, new forms known as Track Warrants and Track Bulletins are issued by the train dispatcher directly to the crews operating the trains.

At terminals, these warrants and bulletins are computer printouts which are given directly to the crew members. At intermediate points along the line, the dispatcher contacts the trains by radio and instructs the crews. Most instructions involve checking particular lines and filling in the blank spaces on the warrant or bulletin forms. The train crew members then repeat the instructions back to the dispatcher over the radio, and the dispatcher checks to be sure the train crew understands the instructions correctly.

Another significant change on the Santa Fe at that time was changing portions of lines previously known as "districts" to the new term (for Santa Fe) "subdivisions."

On May 15, 1988, Santa Fe consolidated many of its divisions and ended up with only six divisions on the entire system. The new California Division comprises the former Los Angeles and Valley Divisions and includes all lines west of Needles (CA) and Parker (AZ). At the same time, subdivisions that were previously numbered (such as First, Second, etc.) were given names instead. Thus the line between Barstow and San Bernardino (with which this volume is concerned), which for many years was known as the First District of the Los Angeles Division, is now known as the Cajon Subdivision of the California Division.

Early in November of 1989, the Santa Fe relocated its former Los Angeles Division headquarters and its Valley Division headquarters from its respective depots in San Bernardino and Fresno into a new California Division Managers office building located in a recently developed commerce center just north of the I-10 freeway near Waterman Avenue in the southern portion of San Bernardino. Trains are now dispatched from a modern dispatching center at this new location.

From August 1981 until April 1989, the Union Pacific stationed a two-unit helper at Victorville. Since then, UP helpers have been based at Colton. The Santa Fe continues to use helpers out of San Bernardino, while the Southern Pacific bases a helper at Dike. On all three railroads, only exceptionally heavy trains require helpers. Present-day helpers are used not only for additional power on upgrades, but also to help retard trains on downgrades through the use of dynamic braking (in which the traction motors become generators and the electrical energy is turned into heat energy by passing through resistance grids).

Perhaps the most obvious change to the train-watcher since 1985 has been the gradual disappearance of cabooses from the rear of freight trains.

While many other things have changed in Cajon Pass since the "good old days" when the author became a train order operator there in 1947, mountain railroading still holds a fascination for many people. It is the author's intention that the photos in this volume will depict to the viewer how it used to be as well as show what it's like today.

WESTWARD ↓				CAJON SUBDIVISION		CAJON SUBDIVISION		EASTWARD ↑		
FIRST CLASS									FIRST CLASS	
35 PSGR	3 PSGR			STATIONS		STATIONS			36 PSGR	4 PSGR
Leave Daily	Leave Daily	Station Number	Siding Feet					Mile Post	Arrive Daily	Arrive Daily
AM 10:27	AM 4:12	19000		BARSTOW — 0.9 — BPRT		BARSTOW — 0.9 — BPRT		745.9	PM s 4:35	PM s11:50
				EAST D YARD — 2.2 —		EAST D YARD — 2.2 —		746.8		
				WEST D YARD — 0.9 —		WEST D YARD — 0.9 —		749.0		
				VALLEY JCT. — 0.9 —		VALLEY JCT. — 0.9 —		749A.0		
				YARD ENTRY — 2.4 —		YARD ENTRY — 2.4 —		4.3		
		19015		LENWOOD — 6.9 —		LENWOOD — 6.9 —		6.7		
				HODGE — 15.8 —		HODGE — 15.8 —		13.6		
				EAST ORO GRANDE — 2.1 —		EAST ORO GRANDE — 2.1 —		29.4		
		19035		ORO GRANDE — 3.1 —		ORO GRANDE — 3.1 —	CTC 2MT	31.5		
				EAST VICTORVILLE — 2.1 —		EAST VICTORVILLE — 2.1 —		34.6		
		19045		VICTORVILLE — 1.3 — P		VICTORVILLE — 1.3 — P		36.7		
				FROST — 7.1 —		FROST — 7.1 —		38.0		
		19055		HESPERIA — 5.0 —		HESPERIA — 5.0 —		45.1		
				LUGO — 5.8 —		LUGO — 5.8 —		50.1		
		19065		SUMMIT — NO. 8.9 — SO. 6.9 —		SUMMIT — NO. 8.9 — SO. 6.9 —		55.9		
		19075		CAJON — 6.6 —		CAJON — 6.6 —		62.8		
		19080		KEENBROOK — 4.5 —		KEENBROOK — 4.5 —		69.4		
				VERDEMONT — 6.9 —		VERDEMONT — 6.9 —		73.9		
				FIFTH STREET — 0.7 —		FIFTH STREET — 0.7 —		80.8		
s12:07 PM	s 6:03 AM	19100		SAN BERNARDINO BPRT		SAN BERNARDINO BPRT		81.5	2:45 PM	10:02 PM
Arrive Daily	Arrive Daily			SOUTH TRACK (82.0) NORTH TRACK (84.0)		SOUTH TRACK (82.0) NORTH TRACK (84.0)			Leave Daily	Leave Daily

Chard Walker

A BRIEF HISTORY

Cajon Canyon, which separates the San Gabriel Mountains to the west from the San Bernardino Mountains to the east, provides the only practical route for railroads through the mountain range separating the coastal plain comprising the greater Los Angeles metropolitan area from the Mojave Desert for many miles in either direction. Cajon (kah-HONE) means "box" in Spanish, and the canyon was given this name due to its box-like configuration with very steep walls and rough terrain along its upper extremities. Although the word "pass" generally refers to the actual summit of a route passing across a ridge, in common usage "Cajon Pass" defines the area from the edge of the plain of the Mojave Desert to the lower end of Cajon Canyon at Devore.

Above: An eastbound Santa Fe freight train with a 3800-class 2-10-2 on the point passes the Ono depot in 1946. The depot was closed within a few months. *Bob McVay*

Opposite above: A westbound train passes the Lugo depot in 1923 after a light snowfall. *C.H. Clevenger* Opposite below: The old three-story hotel (left) and depot at Hesperia are seen on February 18, 1940. Note the train order boards with paddles removed; beyond is the track foreman's house and a garage. The depot was moved to Victorville in 1942, where it became the "roundhouse." *Ralph Melching*

The first railroad to operate over Cajon Pass was the California Southern Railroad, completed in 1885 with Santa Fe backing. From 1897 until 1902 the railroad was known as the Santa Fe Pacific, which today (1989) is again Santa Fe's parent company's "new" name.

Starting in 1905, trains of the Los Angeles and Salt Lake Railroad (now the Union Pacific) began operating over Santa Fe rails through Cajon Pass via a trackage rights agreement which is still in effect.

The original single-track line was built on a 2.2 percent grade from San Bernardino to Cajon station. The final six miles from Cajon to Summit were on a 3 percent grade. When the line was double-tracked between San Bernardino and Summit before World War I, the second track was built on a 2.2 percent grade all the way, with the new serpentine track being two miles longer than the original track between Cajon and Summit. Since the new track was used for eastbound trains going upgrade, while the older track was used only for westbound trains going downgrade, it was necessary for trains to operate left-handed between San Bernardino and Summit.

When double-tracking of the line between Summit and Barstow was completed in 1924, trains continued to operate left-handed all the way from San Bernardino to a point between Thorn and Frost at Milepost 39.1, where the newer track crossed above the original track on a bridge (a "flyover") to enable trains to operate right-handed from there to Barstow and beyond.

In 1967 the Southern Pacific Railroad built a new single-track line from Palmdale through Cajon Pass to West Colton which is fairly close to the Santa Fe tracks between Summit and Devore.

In 1972 the Santa Fe realigned three miles of its route in the Summit area to lower the elevation by 50 feet and reduce curvature. At the same time, centralized traffic control (CTC) was installed over the entire line between San Bernardino and Barstow so that trains can now be operated over both tracks in either direction. Subsequent minor line changes by the Santa Fe have reduced maximum curvature between Cajon and Summit from 10 degrees to six degrees-thirty minutes (6½ degrees).

For a more complete history, the reader is invited to refer to *Cajon—Rail Passage to the Pacific.*

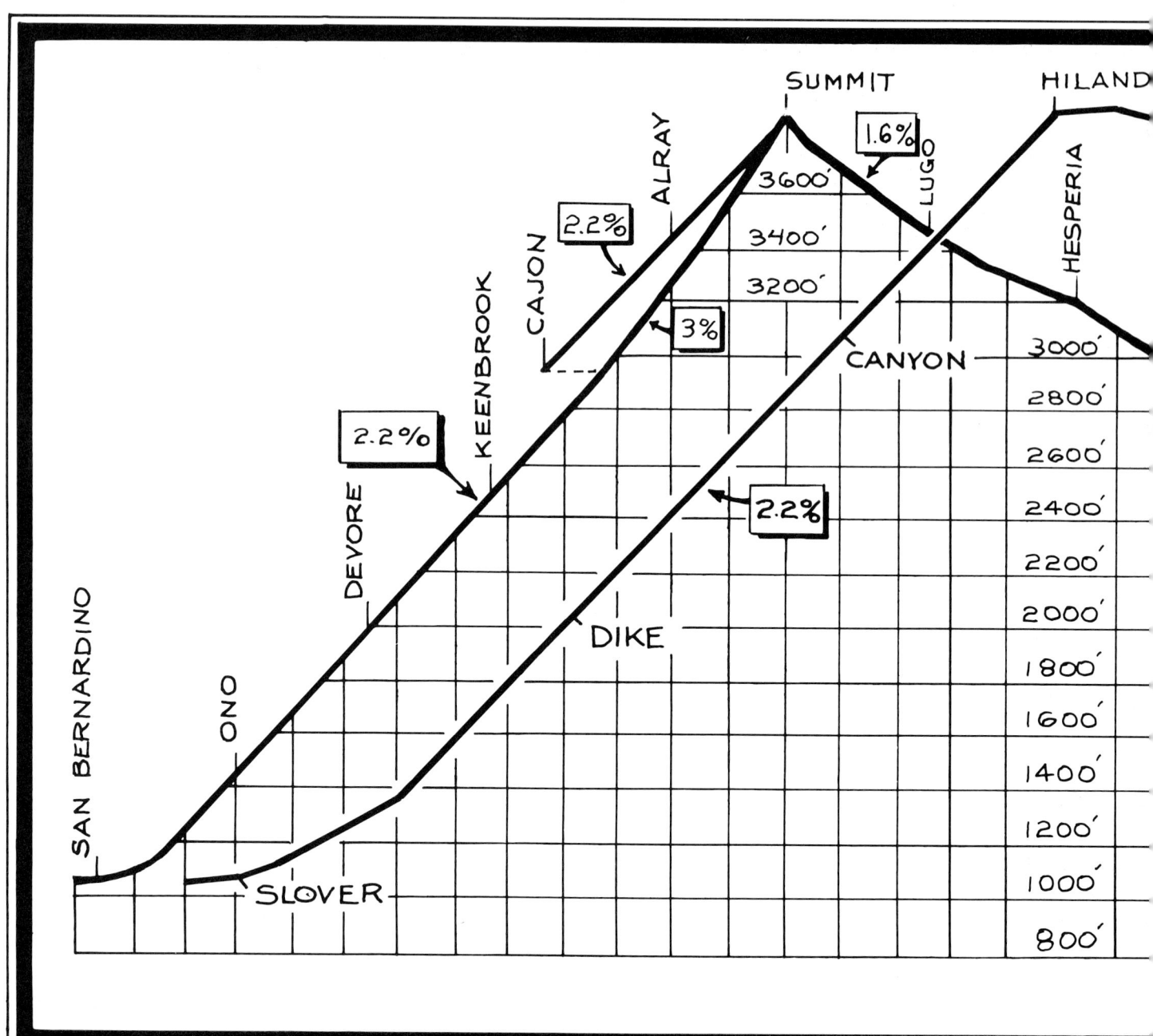

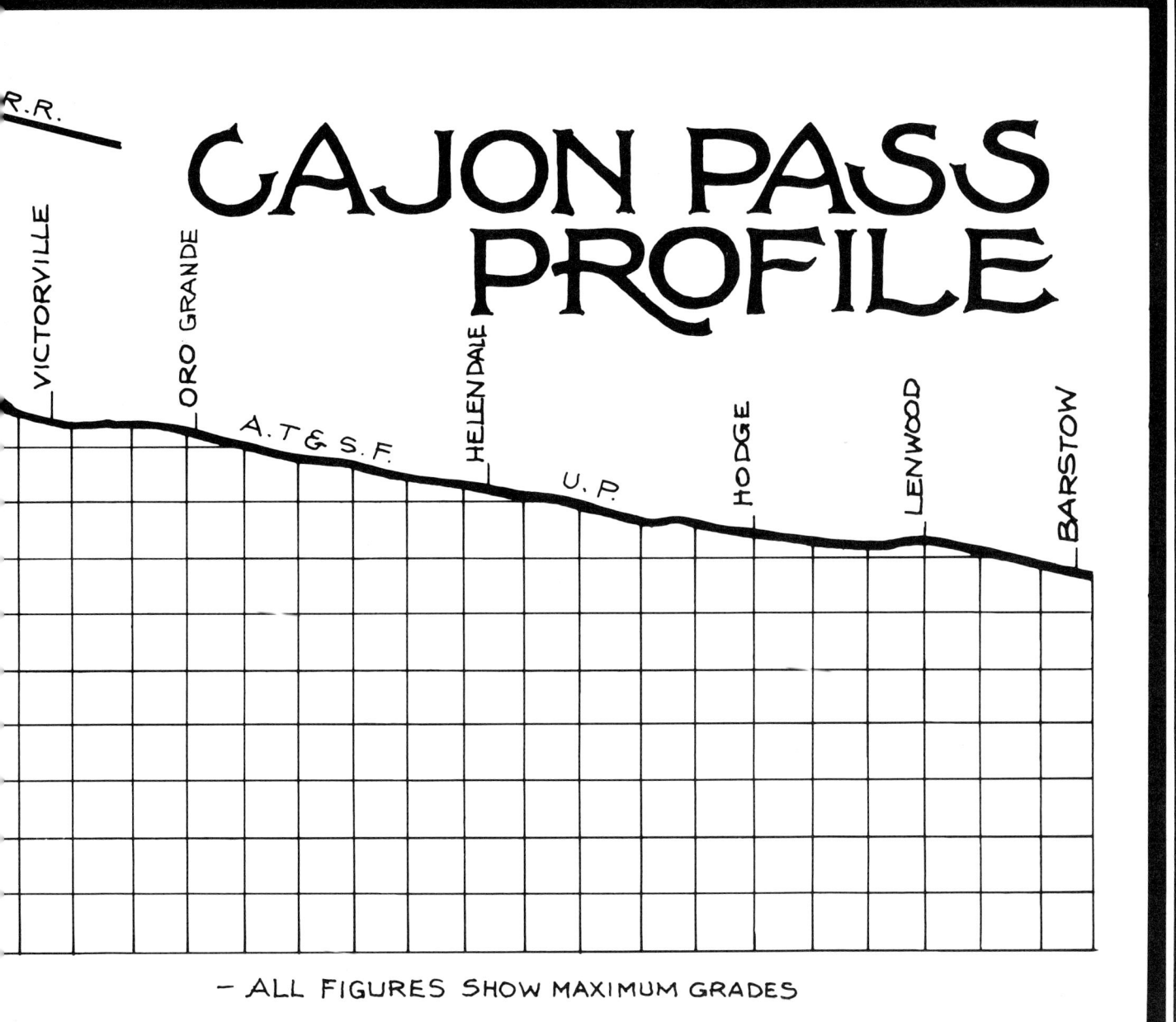

CAJON PASS PROFILE

R.R.

VICTORVILLE

ORO GRANDE

A.T.&S.F.

HELENDALE

U.P.

HODGE

LENWOOD

BARSTOW

— ALL FIGURES SHOW MAXIMUM GRADES

· SAN · BERNARD

First 22, the EL CAPITAN, is ready to leave San Bernardino on December 22, 1940, with road engine 4 (an Electro-Motive E1A) and steam helper 1240. *Francis C. Smith (Stan Kistler Collection)*

Above: GP7s 109 and 106, coupled nose-to-nose, help an eastbound UP passenger train with an Alco PA/PB/PA combination. The location is along I Street in San Bernardino north of Baseline, and the date is April 22, 1954. The six-lane freeway of Interstate 215 now occupies the area of the shed and trees at left. *Lewis Harris* Below: Two Fairbanks-Morse helpers, the 1360 and 1362, shove against the rear of an eastbound freight near Ono in 1950. These units could not be connected in multiple-unit fashion, so each unit had an engineer and a fireman. *Robert Heuerman*

Above: Looking northwest from the second floor of the Santa Fe depot at San Bernardino (which served as headquarters for the Los Angeles Division until November 1989) on October 21, 1949. An eastbound Santa Fe freight with a steam helper ahead of the caboose is leaving town, headed for Cajon Pass. The tall smokestack at right is located at the powerhouse for the Santa Fe shops. In the distance are the San Gabriel Mountains. *Jack Whitmeyer* Below: Santa Fe's only Fairbanks-Morse passenger locomotive has arrived at San Bernardino with train No. 23, the westbound GRAND CANYON LIMITED, in the early 1950s. *Jack Whitmeyer*

Above: Alco RSD15 "alligators" 811, 810 and 809 in their original black and silver paint scheme pull an eastbound Santa Fe freight up the 2.2 percent grade at Ono in June 1959. These units were soon repainted into Santa Fe's blue and yellow scheme. *Donald Sims* Right: U.S. Army 4006, an 0-6-0, working at the quartermaster depot at Ono in May 1947. *Bill Garner* Opposite: An eastbound UP freight near Ono on October 11, 1939, with 2-8-8-0 3531 on the point and 2-8-2 2710 helping. *Two Photos, Richard H. Kindig*

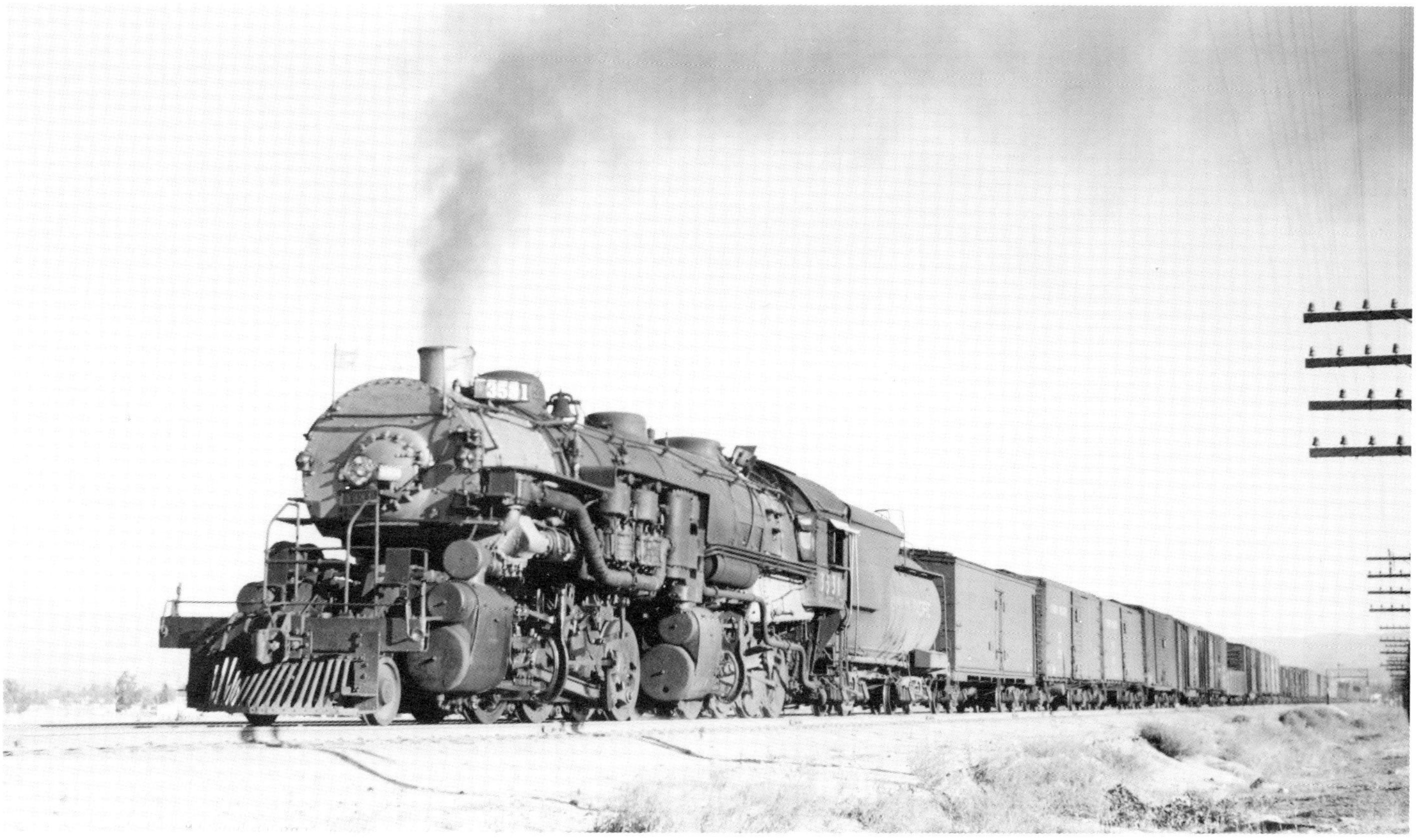

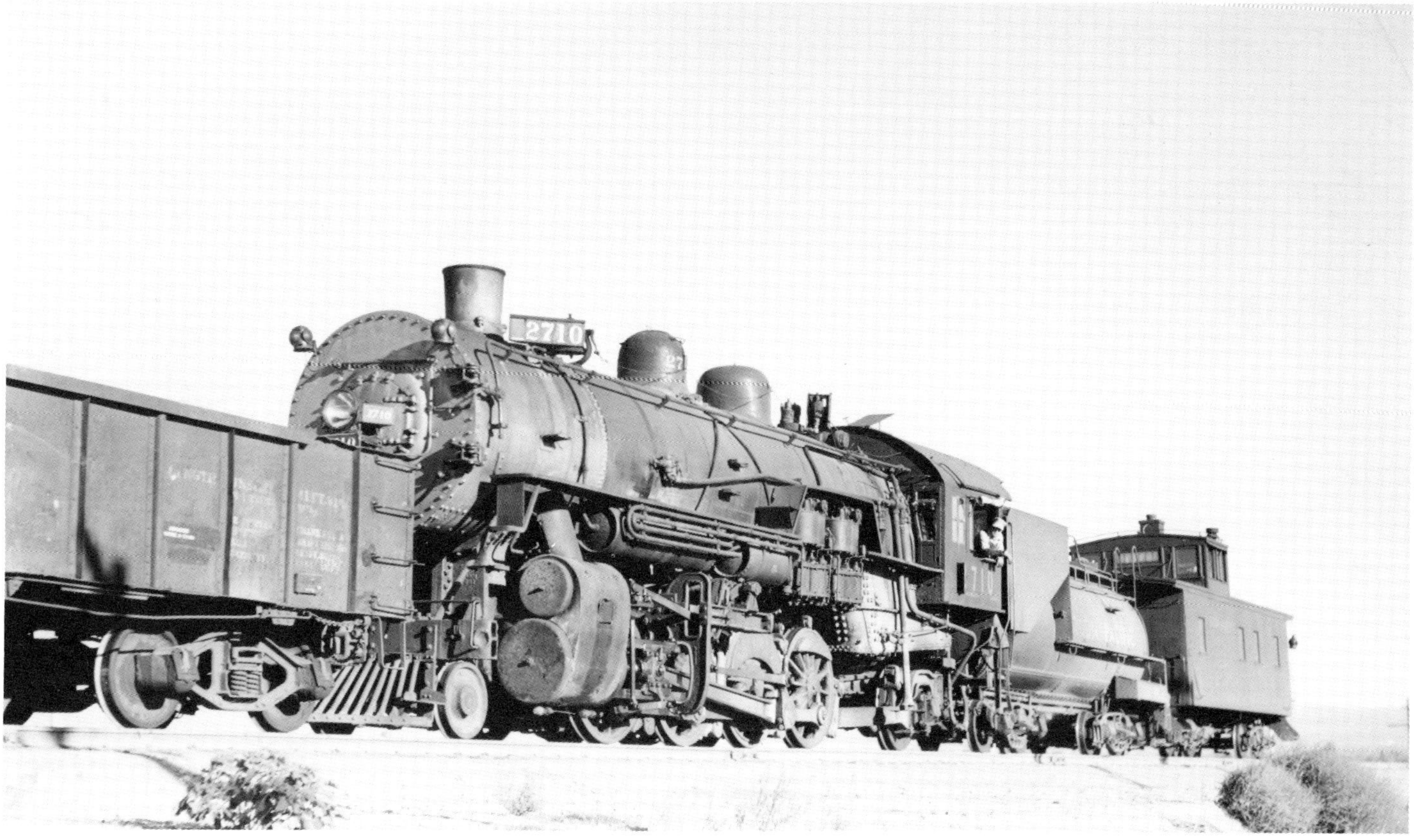
2710

Above: With a trio of E9s in charge, UP train No. 10, the CITY OF ST. LOUIS, pauses at San Bernardino on February 12, 1960. *Allan Styffe*
Below: This Baldwin DT 6-6-2000 center cab unit was normally used on the Kaiser Turn between San Bernardino and Kaiser (on today's Pasadena Subdivision) on weekdays, but on weekends it was sometimes used to help freight trains up Cajon Pass to Summit. It is seen here on January 23, 1953, after returning ''light'' from Summit following a helper job. *Jack Whitmeyer*

Above: This rare scene, taken December 17, 1950, looks north along the switching lead at the east end of the "A" Yard at San Bernardino. At left is the rarely photographed Fifth Street Tower. Engine 1901, a 2-8-0 not usually assigned to this terminal, drifts down the westbound main line with a single boxcar. The San Bernardino Mountains can be seen in the distance on this exceptionally clear day. *Jack Whitmeyer* Below: Union Pacific's eastbound UTAHN is seen just above Highland Avenue leaving San Bernardino on June 11, 1950, with Mountain-type 7019 on the point. *Jack Whitmeyer*

Top: Union Pacific's first gas-turbine locomotive, unit 50, is descending the grade at Devore on March 15, 1950. The 50 was the only turbine with a cab at each end. A caboose was always located immediately behind the locomotive to carry General Electric and UP personnel who were constantly monitoring the turbine's performance. *Thomas Hotchkiss (Author's Collection)* Above left: UP No. 717, the westbound CHALLENGER with 4-6-6-4 3935 on the point, descends the grade between Ono and San Bernardino on a bright June morning in 1940. Note the semaphore signal on the distant signal bridge. The engines in this class were later renumbered into the 3800 series. *Walt Thrall (John Shaw Collection)* Above right: Santa Fe Northern 3759 leads No. 19, the westbound CHIEF, just below Devore on October 16, 1939. *Frank Peterson (Bob Kern Collection)*

Opposite top: Union Pacific's Oro Grande Turn climbs the grade at Ono behind 2-8-2 type engine 2264 on November 1, 1941. Standing at the far left is well-known photographer Dick Kindig, who spent two days chasing trains in the pass with Frank Peterson. Dick supplies additional data: The train had 11 cars, was moving about 30 mph, and the time was 8:11 A.M. *Frank Peterson (Bob Kern Collection)* Opposite below: First 17, the hi-level EL CAPITAN, is seen near the lower end of Devore siding in July 1967. Note the typical Santa Fe phone booth at left, and beyond it the new SP line. *Thomas Hotchkiss (Author's Collection)*

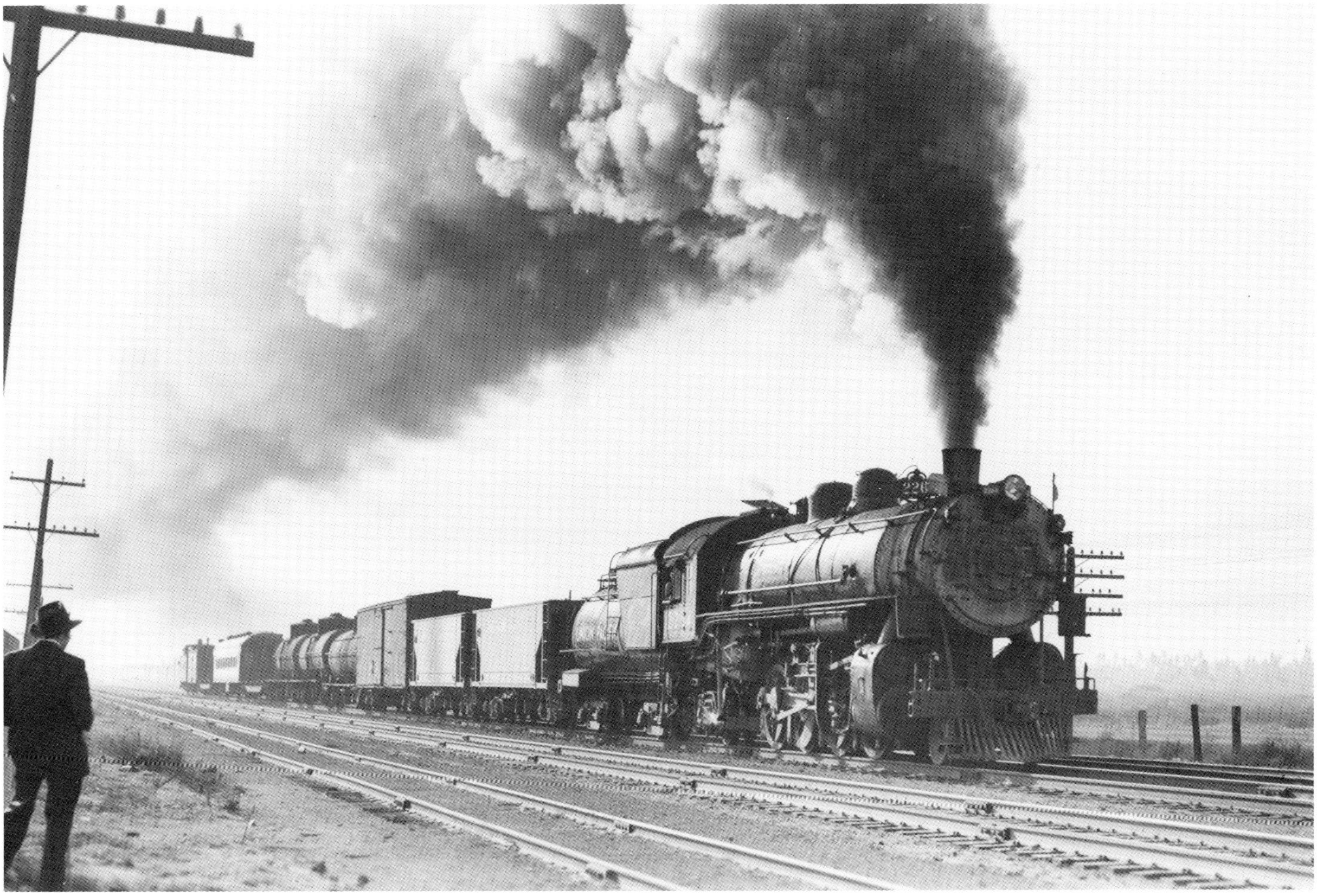

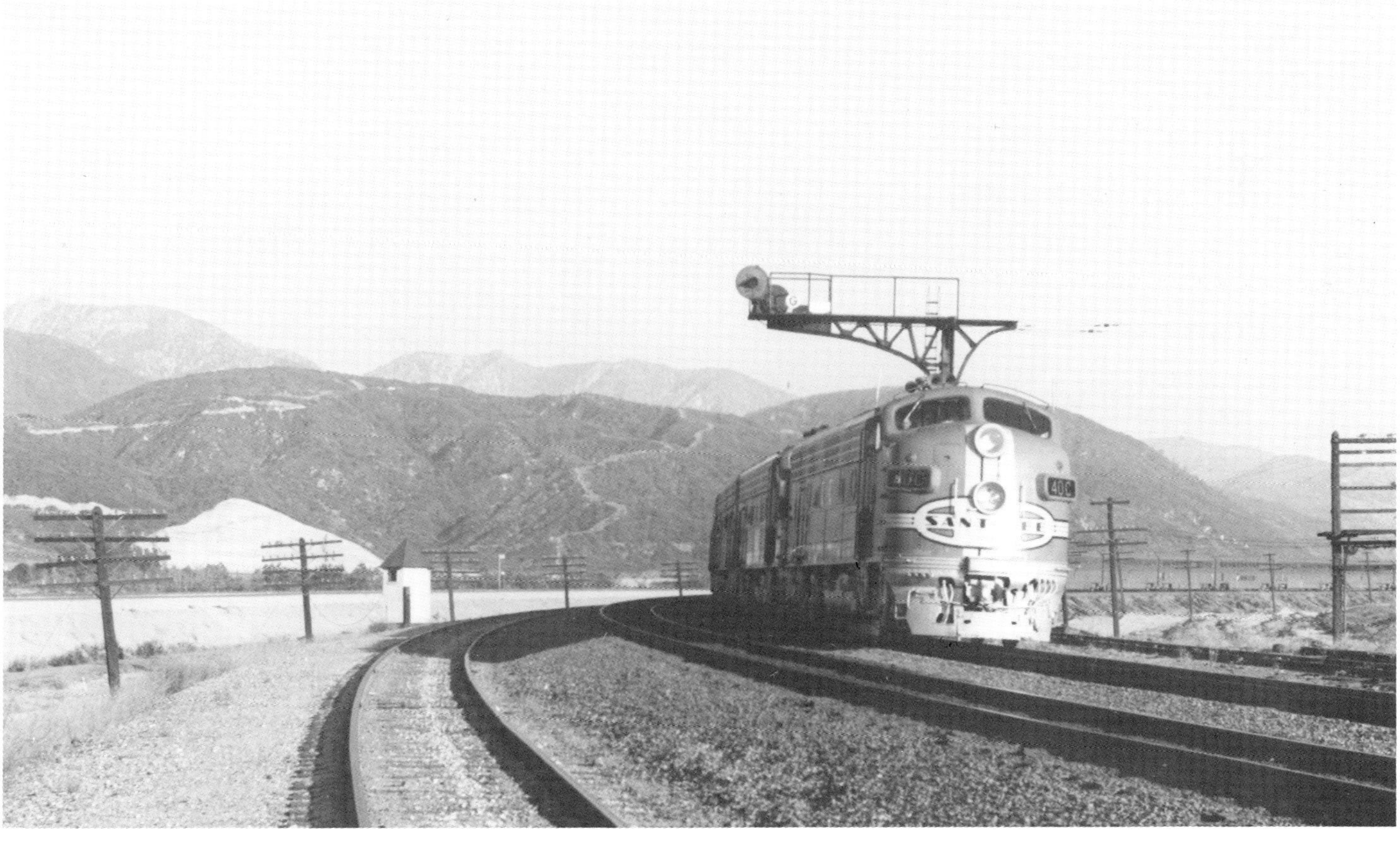

Above: AT&SF Extra 3889 East has yet another 2-10-2 type helper on the point on June 11, 1952. This was the last year that Santa Fe used steam on freight trains and as helpers during the annual ''spud rush'' in June. The train is seen here at Ono. *Jack Whitmeyer* Below: A Southern Pacific train led by SD45-rebuilt 7399, wearing an experimental DAYLIGHT paint scheme, crosses the high bridge over Lytle Creek between Bench and Dike in January 1982. The train is heading upgrade from SP's West Colton classification yard, and is westbound by timetable direction. *David R. Busse*

Above: An eastbound Santa Fe train with SD39s, 1570, 1562, 1556, 1574 and SDF45 5955 crosses above Cajon Blvd. between Verdemont and Devore on January 18, 1986. All units except the 1556 are painted in the anticipated-but-never-realized AT&SF-SP merger scheme—sometimes referred to by railfans as "Kodachromes." *Mike Lepker.* Left: In 1989 Cargill Grain Co. opened a bulk grain distribution plant between Verdemont and Devore. This ex-SP EMD NW2 is used to switch the covered hoppers that bring the grain from the midwest. *Elrond G. Lawrence*

Above: Santa Fe helpers 3013 (a 2-10-2) and 3723 (a 4-8-2) at the rear of an eastward freight at Devore in August 1947. *James Ady* Below: An eastbound SP freight crosses Cajon Creek just above Dike in January 1974. At the far right is the Santa Fe's bridge. *David Styffe*

Top: Santa Fe FP45 102, in its original "warbonnet" red and stainless-steel color scheme, brings the last remnant of the GRAND CANYON up the grade at Devore on February 3, 1968, just a few days before this train was abolished. The 102 was later repainted into Santa Fe's blue and yellow freight scheme and renumbered 5942, and then 5992. In 1989 it was returned to its original red and silver colors, and became "Super Fleet" 101. *Thomas Hotchkiss (Author's Collection)* Above: No. 22, the EL CAPITAN, at Devore in the early 1950s before this train was equipped with hi-level cars. *Santa Fe Photo by R. Collins Bradley*

Above: Union Pacific 2823 West rolls through the curves west of Devore on January 25, 1973. Note the 1970s-era "Dependable Transportation" lettering worn by lead U30C 2823, as it leads a brace of GE power on this overcast day. *Dick Stephenson* Above Right: Santa Fe SD26 4617 leads a fellow SD24 rebuild through Devore on a crisp and clear February 3, 1979 morning. *Allan Styffe* Below Right: A westbound AT&SF freight with units 5959, 5654, 9513 and 5025 crosses Cajon Creek just above Devore on January 3, 1986. *Mike Lepker*

·DEVORE·TO·SUI

Amtrak train No. 3, the westbound SOUTHWEST LIMITED (now the SOUTHWEST CHIEF) with SDP40F units 506, 619, 533 at the new location of Keenbrook on June 18, 1976. Inset: Fairbanks-Morse unit 1366 helps an eastbound UP passenger train powered by Alco PA/PBs just above Keenbrook near Milepost 68, around 1949. *Both Photos, Thomas Hotchkiss (Author's Collection)*

LIVAN'S · CURVE ·

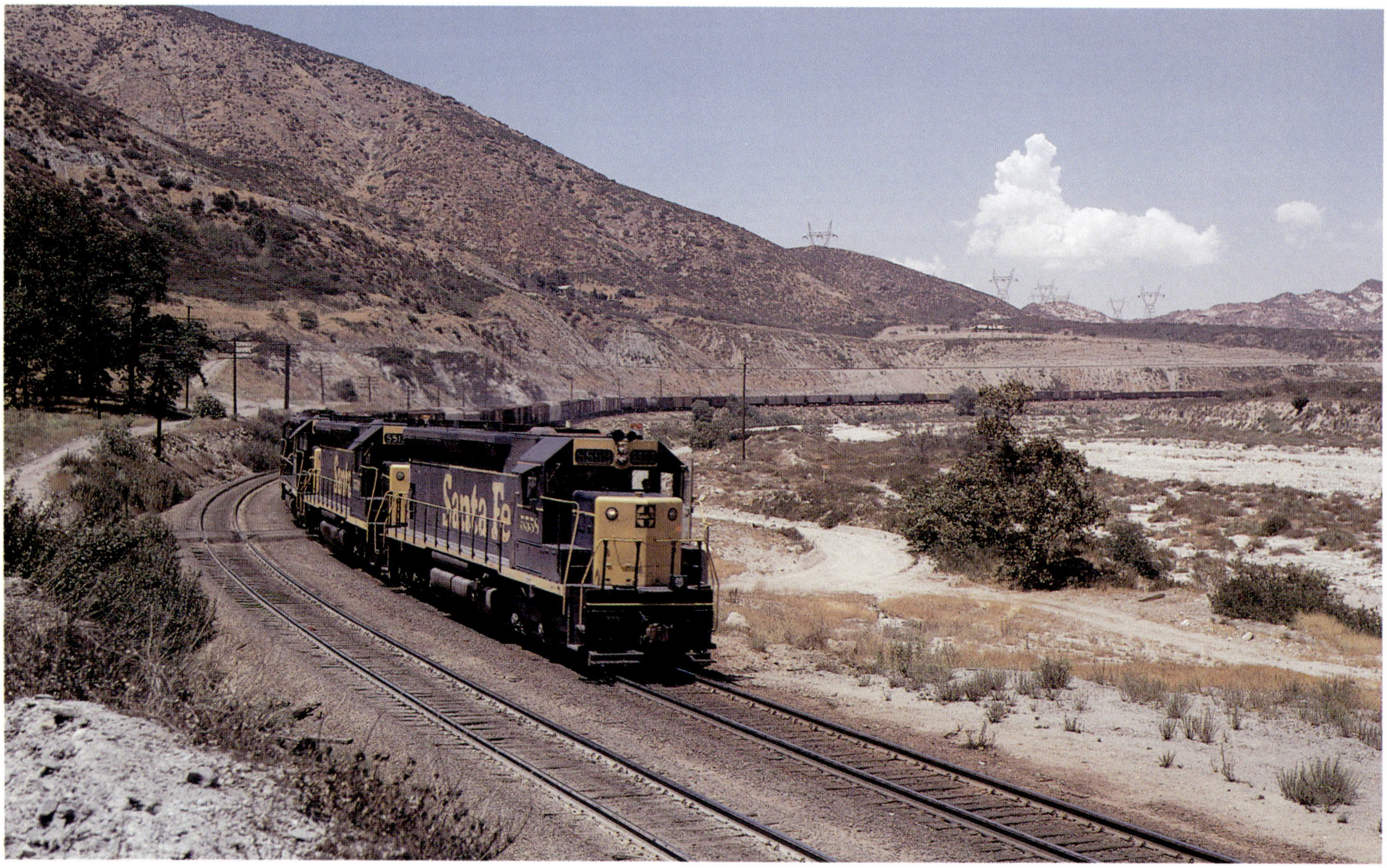
Santa Fe

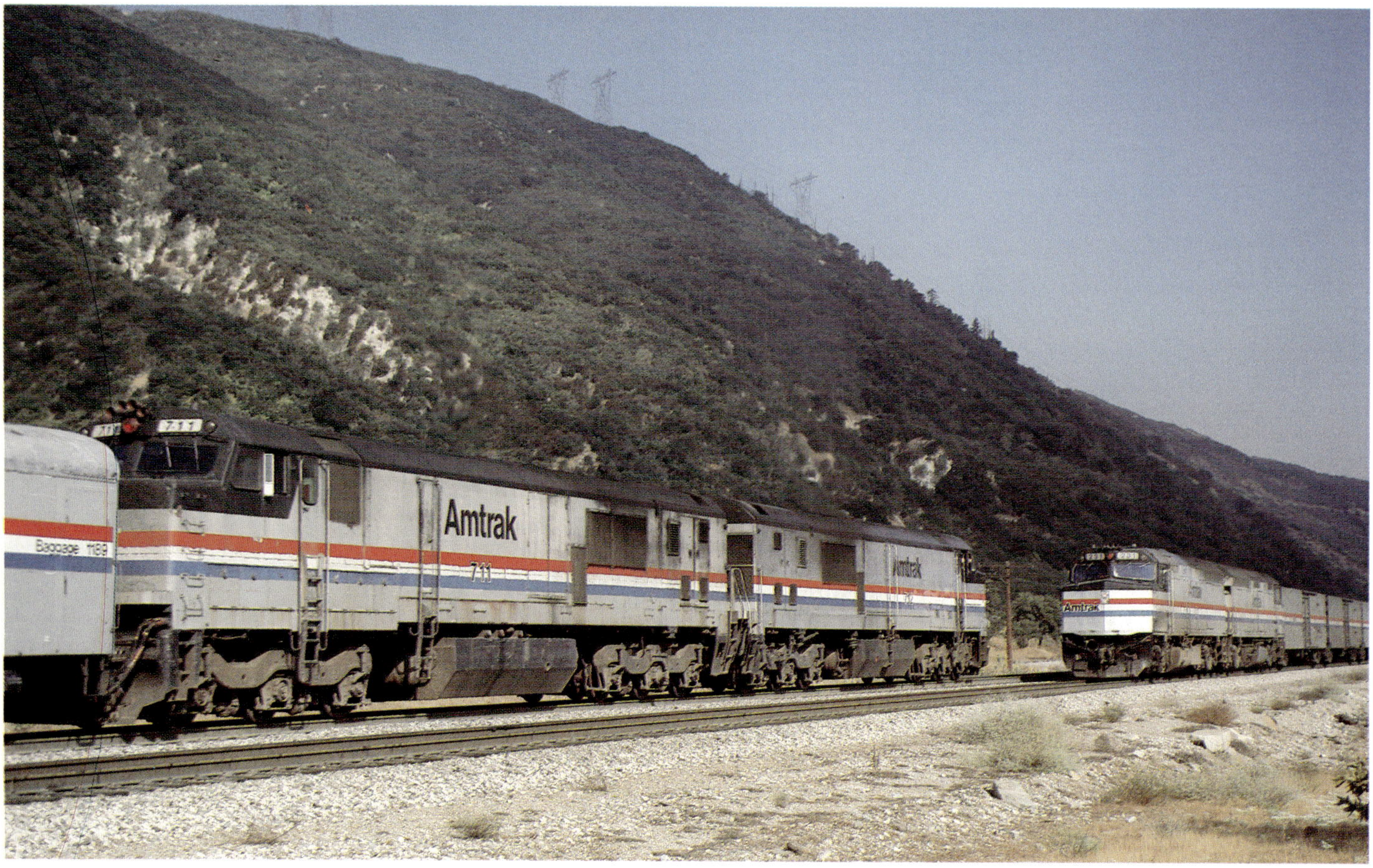
Amtrak
Baggage 1189
711
Amtrak
Amtrak

Above Left: Santa Fe Extra 5558 West descends the grade just above Keenbrook in July 1974. *Chard L. Walker* Bottom Left: An extremely rare meet of two Amtrak trains took place near the new location of Keenbrook on July 8, 1989. At left is train No. 2, the eastbound SUNSET LIMITED, which is detouring over Santa Fe rails from Colton to Phoenix because of a derailment on the SP's Sunset Route. At the right is train No. 3, the westbound SOUTHWEST CHIEF, running almost three hours late. When Santa Fe installed CTC in 1972, Keenbrook was relocated three miles lower to MP 69.4, from its original location west of MP 66. *Rod Higbie* Above: In the mid-1980s a westbound Santa Fe train passes a Union Pacific freight on the big curve below Blue Cut. This view looks southwest. *Richard Steinheimer*

Top: An eastward Santa Fe freight climbs upgrade beside a west-bound SP train near Keenbrook on a hazy day in the early 1970s. *Richard Steinheimer* Above: Santa Fe's only Fairbanks-Morse passenger diesel was the 90, a three-unit set. Here it is at Keenbrook with No. 23, the westbound GRAND CANYON, on April 10, 1954. *Thomas Hotchkiss (Author's Collection)*

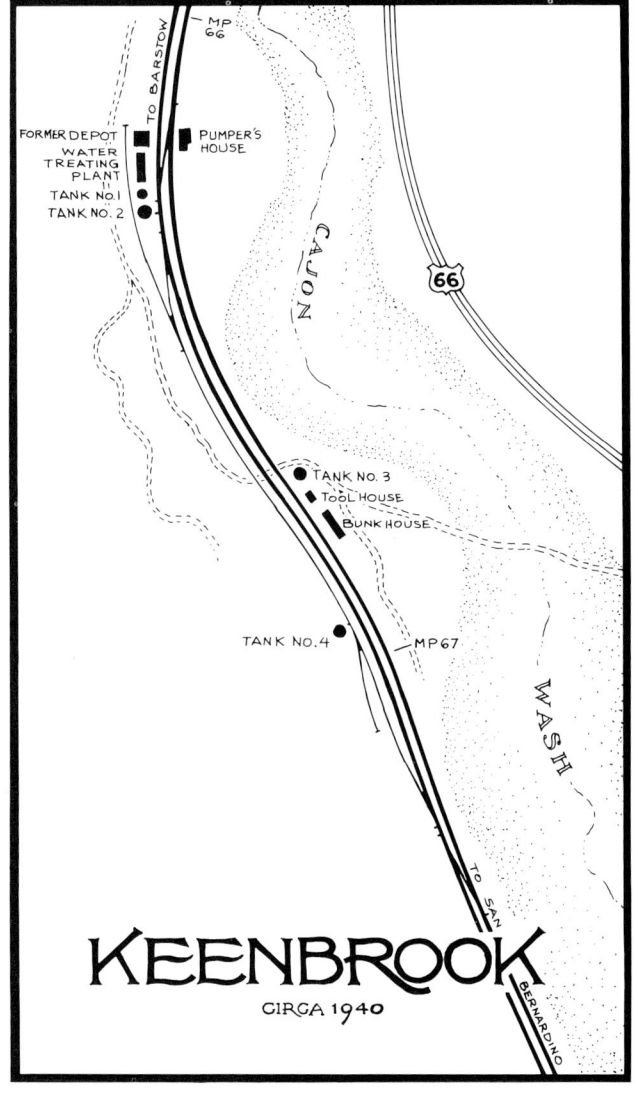

Top: Santa Fe 3876 leads a westbound freight below Keenbrook in the 1940s. The rugged 2-10-2s of this class were Santa Fe's backbone of freight power before FTs intruded. *Thomas Hotchkiss (Author's Collection)* Above: A westbound SP freight with SD35 6905 on the point climbs the grade at Milepost 478 between Dike and Canyon on April 28, 1968. *John Shaw*

Above: Amtrak's Rohr Turbotrain, heading east on a deadhead move, passes through Blue Cut on July 17, 1976. *Dick Stephenson* Below: Newly repainted and renumbered Santa Fe SDFP45s 100 and 101 power a three-car special passenger train through Blue Cut on August 22, 1989. The train carried AT&SF and Los Angeles County officials to the Mojave Desert town of Amboy, to look over a proposed trash-by-rail route and disposal site. *Elrond G. Lawrence* Union Pacific is famous for its "Unlimited Power" lashups, and in this trio of images at Blue Cut, it's easy to understand why. Above: An eastbound LAX climbs the hill with an incredible assortment of power: three SD40-2s, a Norfolk & Western GE, two BN SD units and a DDA40X Centennial! Two yellow business cars round out the head end on this April 15, 1979 day. *Ed Chapman; Dick Stephenson collection* Below: UP and C&NW SD40-2s lead a westbound American President Lines' doublestack train over the Blue Cut arch in September 1985. *Bob Kern* Finally (bottom), we see an eastbound grain extra on June 2, 1979, led by SD45 40 and a DD35B/DD35 combination. *Mike Lepker*

Above: Number 204 (UP No. 4, the eastbound UTAHN) with road engine 814 (a 4-8-4) and helper 5098 (a 4-10-2) at Blue Cut on November 9, 1947. *Fred Hust* Right: Union Pacific 4-6-6-4 3981 leads the westbound PONY EXPRESS below Cajon on August 12, 1947. The train was several hours late that day, as it was scheduled to operate over Cajon both ways at night. *James Ady*

Opposite: Two views of the eastbound EL CAPITAN at Blue Cut in 1955, when it had a full-length dome car, but before the advent of hi-level cars. *Two Photos, Robert Heuerman*

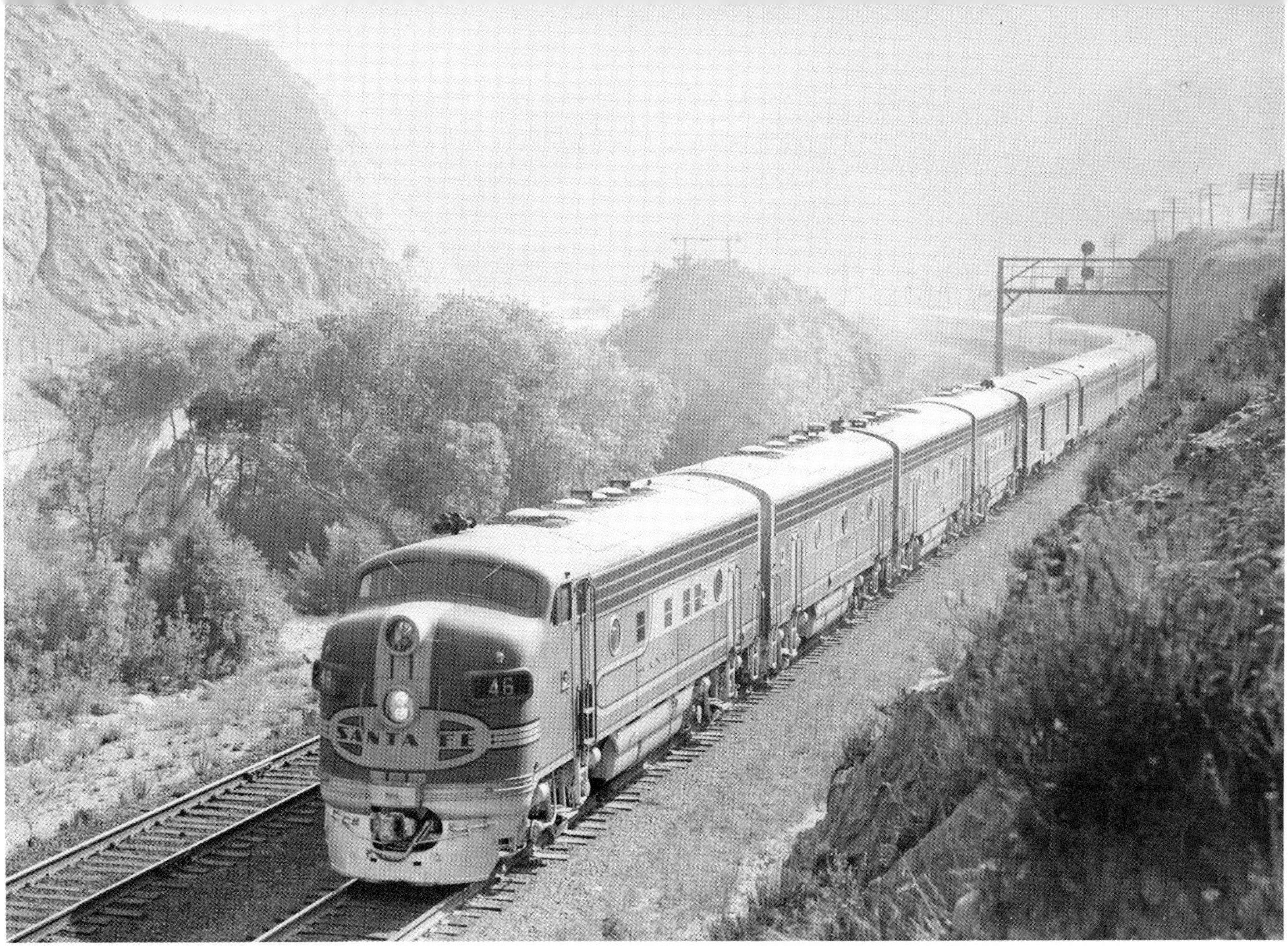
46
SANTA FE

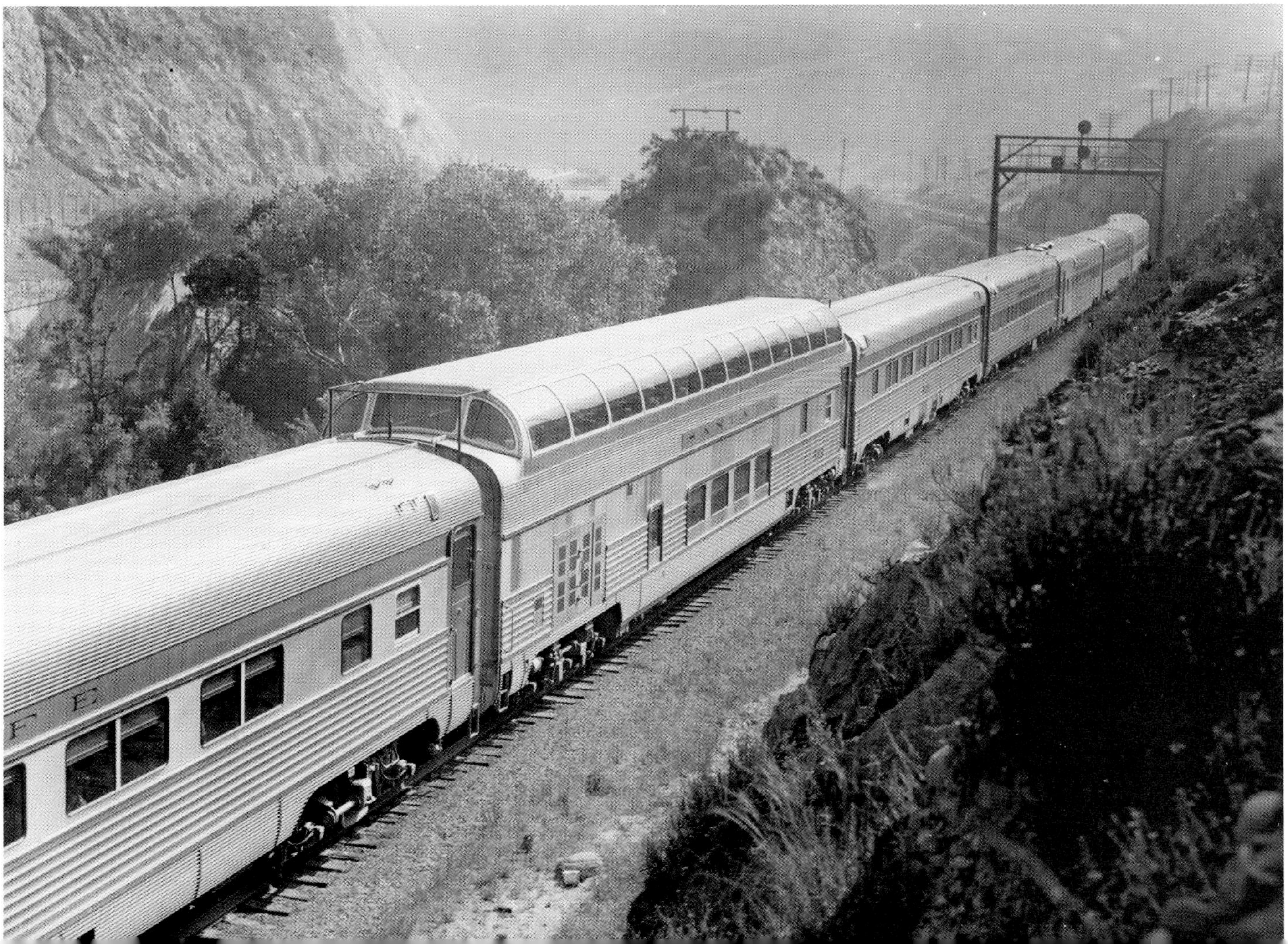

Above: Amtrak No. 3, the westbound SOUTHWEST LIMITED led by SDP40F 516, passes an AT&SF freight at Blue Cut on October 6, 1979. *Steve Gartner; Dick Stephenson collection* Bottom Left: This eastbound Santa Fe train has four cowl units painted in the AT&SF-SP ''Kodachrome'' merger scheme, and is seen at Blue Cut on February 15, 1986. *Mike Lepker* Above Left: Ex-SP E9A 6051 is seen running light through the Blue Cut area on May 12, 1988. The streamlined unit is on its way back to its home at the California State Railroad Museum in Sacramento, after being displayed at the San Diego Railroad Fair. *Elrond G. Lawrence*

An eastbound Union Pacific freight ascends the grade on the portion of the line that was relocated to the west side of Cajon Creek in 1939. The original line was on the far side of the creek at the left. In this January 1967 view, grading work for the new SP line is just getting under way on the hillside at right. *Thomas Hotchkiss (Author's Collection)*

AT&SF 3892, a 2-10-2, leads an eastbound freight near the lower end of Cajon siding in the late 1940s. *Thomas Hotchkiss (Author's Collection)*

Above: UP train No. 104, the eastbound CITY OF LOS ANGELES, rolls through Cajon on March 5, 1970, with a trio of E-units in charge of the long yellow train. *Allan Styffe* Below: Union Pacific 279 East passes the old Cajon Station in April 1955, led by a GP9 and two cabless sisters. *Bob Kern*

Above: On April 12, 1986, Santa Fe operated a special passenger train from Los Angeles to Barstow and return to commemorate 100 years of service between the two points—as well as ten years since the opening of AT&SF's Barstow classification yard. The train, featuring both Santa Fe and Amtrak equipment, is shown stopped at Cajon siding while a brief ceremony was held on the west side of the train. Lead unit 5998 was returned to its blue and yellow freight scheme in 1987; in 1989 the unit returned to its original red and silver colors, and was renumbered 102. *Jim Minor* Below: A single GE unit, U36C-rebuild 9500, leads a westbound hotshot "Q" train (the Q stands for quality service) through Cajon on December 20, 1987. *Elrond G. Lawrence*

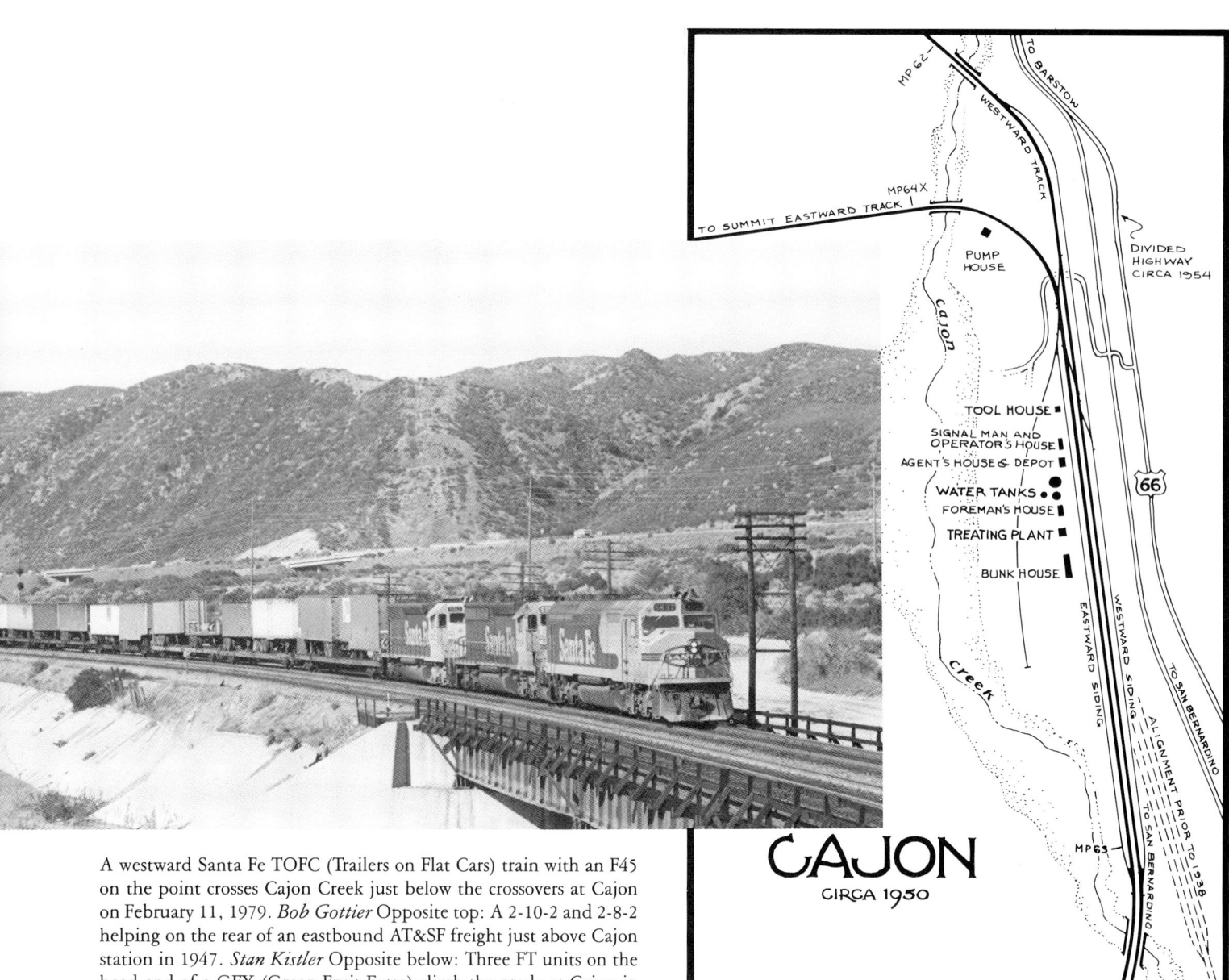

A westward Santa Fe TOFC (Trailers on Flat Cars) train with an F45 on the point crosses Cajon Creek just below the crossovers at Cajon on February 11, 1979. *Bob Gottier* Opposite top: A 2-10-2 and 2-8-2 helping on the rear of an eastbound AT&SF freight just above Cajon station in 1947. *Stan Kistler* Opposite below: Three FT units on the head end of a GFX (Green Fruit Extra) climb the grade at Cajon in the late 1940s. *Stan Kistler*

CAJON

CIRCA 1950

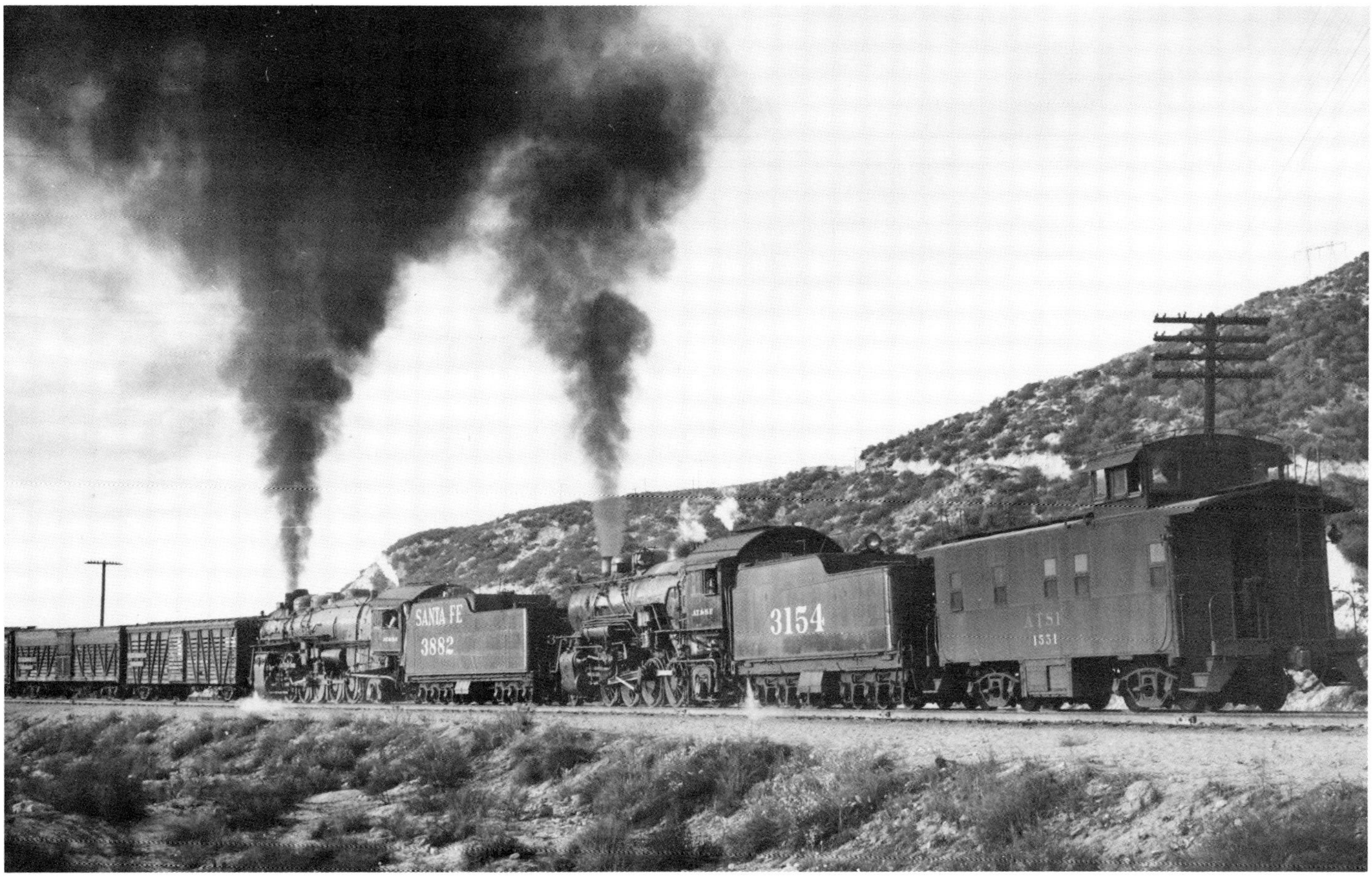
SANTA FE
3882
3154

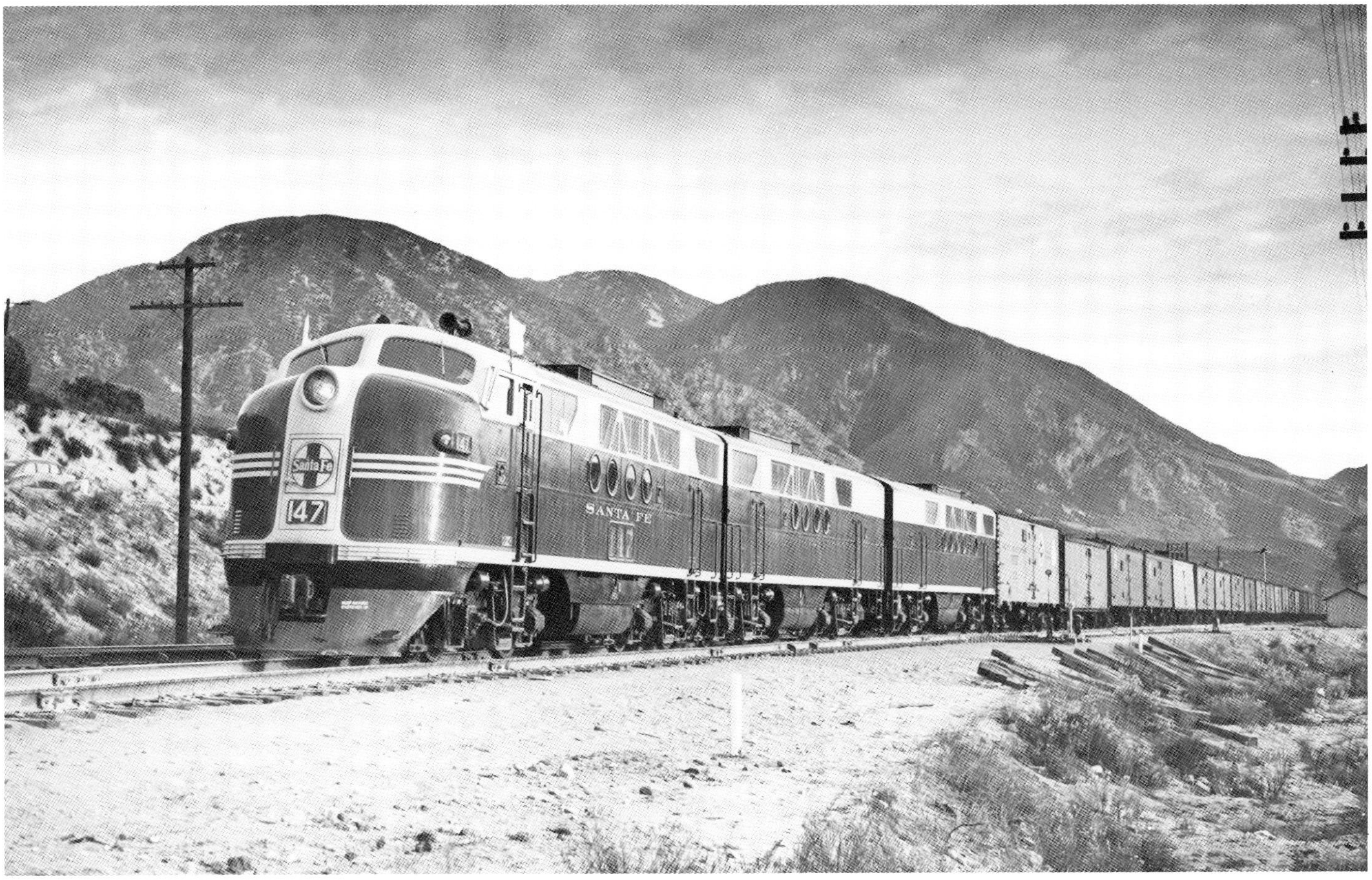
Santa Fe
147
SANTA FE

Top: Second 104, the eastbound CHALLENGER, passes Cajon in 1964. *Thomas Hotchkiss (Author's Collection)* Above: Santa Fe No. 20, the CHIEF, passes Cajon station in 1950. The track at left is the eastward siding. *Robert Heuerman*

Above: A westward SP train with an SD40T-2 ''tunnel motor'' on the point approaches Sullivan's Curve in December 1974. *Henry Brueckman* Left: Seaboard Coast Line GEs 1851 and 1855 bracket slug 3215 at MP 471, approaching Sullivan's Curve on November 26, 1977. The SCL units were borrowed by SP for testing; they're followed by an SP dynamometer car, and two SP units. *Ed Chapman (Dick Stephenson Collection)*

Top: Union Pacific's PACIFIC LIMITED approaches Sullivan's Curve on November 1, 1941, with 4-8-4 road engine 7852 and helper 2-8-2 2735. *R.H. Kindig* Above: No. 10, the NAVAJO, eastbound just below Sullivan's Curve on May 27, 1939. The Cajon station complex is visible just above the locomotive. *Frank Peterson (Bob Kern Collection)*

Top: AT&SF 1798 helps a diesel-powered passenger train at Cajon while a steam-powered eastbound freight waits in the siding circa 1946. The 1798 and 1799 were the only engines of their class, and were originally 2-8-8-2 compounds 1700 and 1701. They were then rebuilt into 2-8-2s and renumbered in 1924. *Fletcher Swan* Above: A westbound Shriners' Special running as Second No. 3, with 4-8-4 engines 2907 and 2906, passes Cajon on June 19, 1950. *James Ady*

Super power at a super location: UP Dash 8-40C 9167 and SD60 6001 lead an eastbound coal extra around Sullivan's Curve on May 8, 1989. *Bob Finan*

Above: First 20, the eastbound CHIEF, passing through the rock cut between Cajon and Sullivan's Curve on July 25, 1953. *Robert Heuerman* Right: Second 24, a section of the eastbound GRAND CANYON, crossing Cajon Creek just above Cajon in the late 1940s, with Alco PA and PB units. The derrick structure was on a pump house over a well which supplied engine water at Cajon and Keenbrook. In the background below the highway is the westward track on the three percent grade. *Stan Kistler*

Opposite: A westbound Santa Fe trailer train comes down the north track below Sullivan's Curve while a westbound-by-timetable Southern Pacific freight climbs the grade above the lower switch of Canyon siding, as it heads east toward the desert. Part of Santa Fe's north track is visible just below the SP track. *Richard Steinheimer*

Above: On a clear summer day in August 1984, two AT&SF trains pass each other at the upper end of Cajon siding where the two main lines separate. The eastbound train at the left will travel eight miles on a 2.2 percent grade to Summit on the north track, while the westbound train at the right has come six miles from Summit on a 3 percent grade down the south track. *David R. Busse* Below: Zebra-striped GP9 2692 helps an eastbound Santa Fe freight up the north track as it enters Sullivan's Curve in April 1955. *Bob Kern*

Above: Train No. 22, the eastbound EL CAPITAN, rounds Sullivan's Curve on July 16, 1950. *Jack Whitmeyer* Below: The first railfan passenger special operated over the SP's Palmdale Cutoff was chartered by the Pacific Railroad Society on October 22, 1983. The train is seen here above Sullivan's Curve with SP helper 7384 ahead of two Amtrak F40s. The helper SD40R was cut off from the train at Hiland siding. *David R. Busse*

Top: Santa Fe's eastbound GRAND CANYON LIMITED on Sullivan's Curve in the 1930s with road engine 3758 (4-8-4) and helper 1226 (4-6-2). *Herb Sullivan (Trains Magazine Collection)* Above: Santa Fe 3757 (4-8-4) and helper 1226 (4-6-2) with an eastward passenger train on Sullivan's Curve in the 1930s. *Herb Sullivan (Trains Magazine Collection)*

Below: An eastbound Union Pacific freight with 2-10-2 engine 5525 approaches Sullivan's Curve in 1947. *Frank Peterson (Bob Kern Collection)* Left: The legendary train photographer Herb Sullivan poses with his giant camera by the rocks above the curve that now bears his name, probably in the 1930s. *Trains Magazine Collection*

On February 20, 1985, two SP trains are about to meet at Canyon siding while an AT&SF container train negotiates Sullivan's Curve. The curve's 1977 line change reduced curvature from 10 degrees (see the old line at left) to six degrees, 30 minutes. *Richard Steinheimer*

Above: Number 124, the "northern" section of the Grand Canyon that ran via La Junta, Colorado, with 4-8-4s 3759 and 2929 on Sullivan's Curve on August 27, 1951. *Chard L. Walker* Below: AT&SF 2922 (4-8-4) and a diesel doublehead the eastbound Grand Canyon around Sullivan's Curve in the early 1950s. The two light-colored cars at the left were heavyweights painted to look like lightweights with fluted sides. *Thomas Hotchkiss (Author's Collection)*

Above: While the 11 FTs in the 158–168 series were temporarily in passenger service during the late 1940s, they powered most of the diesel-hauled passenger trains over Cajon Pass. Here the 162 is leading First 24, a section of the GRAND CANYON on Sullivan's Curve. *Thomas Hotchkiss (Author's Collection)*

Below: Alco PA 71 is on the point of a section of No. 24, the eastbound GRAND CANYON, on Sullivan's Curve in the 1950s. *Thomas Hotchkiss (Author's Collection)*

Above: Looking southeast from a hill between Sullivan's Curve and Pine Lodge, this December 1966 view shows the new SP grade under construction in the foreground . . . while Santa Fe's eastbound CHIEF passes by on the north track. A portion of the westbound track is visible in the distance. *Chard L. Walker* Below: UP engine 7019, a 4-8-2, powers the local known as the "Leon Turn" past Pine Lodge on July 17, 1950. *Chard L. Walker*

Above: Santa Fe train No. 124, the northern section of the GRAND CANYON LIMITED, passes the long-abandoned lime plant at Pine Lodge in July 1950. *Chard L. Walker* Below: An eastbound Union Pacific train with a Rio Grande SD45 (5338) is shown assisting a Santa Fe train up the grade at Pine Lodge in June 1974. *Mike Lepker*

Opposite: An eastbound Southern Pacific train passes an eastbound AT&SF freight going in the opposite direction just above Sullivan's Curve in the 1970s. The SP track at the lower left is Canyon siding. Note the last two units on the AT&SF train are DIT (dead-in-tow) and have their exhaust stacks covered. *Richard Steinheimer* Above: Santa Fe's eastbound CHIEF ascends the 2.2 percent grade between Sullivan's Curve and Pine Lodge on January 16, 1938, with 4-8-2 road engine 3744 and 2-10-2 helper 3905. The westbound track is hidden by the brush. The flood of March 2, 1938, considerably changed the appearance of the area in the vicinity of Cajon Creek; most of the brush disappeared, and the westward track was afterward protected by riprap or sloping concrete retaining walls. The mountain above the locomotives is Ralston Peak. *Lewis Harris*

Above: Santa Fe No. 22, the EL CAPITAN, with F3A 26 above Sullivan's Curve, 1951. At the left is the westward track, and in the left distance is Cajon station with its water tanks. *Robert Hale*

At Left: Union Pacific 9309, a Dash 8-40C, descends the south track with a westbound APL doublestack train on July 2, 1989. The train is just east of Cajon on this clear and sunny day, as it crosses over Cajon Creek. *Randy Keller* Above: An eastbound Union Pacific LANP (Los Angeles–North Platte) train, led by C30-7 2514, approaches Sullivan's Curve on the north track on May 18, 1989. *Alex Mayes* Below: On July 12, 1986, this westbound AT&SF train sporting four "Kodachrome" units is about to pass under Highway 138 at Pine Lodge. A portion of the old highway can be seen to the right, while the Mormon Rocks loom in the distance. *David R. Busse*

A spectacular view of the Cajon station and Pine Lodge area, as seen from the shoulder of Cleghorn Mountain in 1951. Cajon is seen at the lower left; an eastbound Union Pacific freight with carbody-type diesel helpers just ahead of the caboose has completed going around Sullivan's Curve. At the right, Highway 138 crosses both tracks. Just to the left of the highway between the westward and eastward tracks can be seen a faint trace of the crossover tracks that connected the main tracks until 1948 at Pine Lodge.   *Robert Hale*

Top: Union Pacific 5099, a 4-10-2, helps an eastward passenger train near Pine Lodge in 1947. Although the early-style diesel units have "City of Los Angeles" painted on their flanks, some of the cars are heavyweights and are not painted in "streamliner yellow." *Lewis Harris* Above: A Union Pacific stock train is seen descending the three percent grade below Pine Lodge in 1970. The units powering the train consist of SD24 402, SD40s 3060 and 3007, and DD35 81. *Thomas Hotchkiss (Author's Collection)*

Top: Santa Fe 1346 (4-6-2) and 3767 (4-8-4) with an eastward passenger train on the curve above Cajon in the 1940s. *Fletcher Swan* Above: Second 24, a section of the Grand Canyon, with 4-8-4 2929 in a fresh coat of paint, is seen at Pine Lodge in 1948. *James Ady*

Above: An eastbound Southern Pacific freight with the company's lowest numbered SD45, unit 8800, on the point drifts downgrade past the Mormon Rocks at Canyon siding in December 1972. *Richard Steinheimer* Left: Union Pacific 3555, a 2-8-8-0, on the head end of an eastward freight passing Milepost 60x at Alray in the mid-1940s. Above the engine's tender is snow-covered Mt. San Antonio, better known as "Old Baldy." *Thomas Hotchkiss (Author's Collection)*

Above: Engine 3868 leads an eastbound freight near Pine Lodge in September 1947. *Frank Peterson (Bob Kern Collection)* Below: An eastbound Union Pacific piggyback train below Alray in January 1973. The Southern Pacific line can be seen at the left. *Union Pacific Railroad*

Above: Southern Pacific TE70-4S units 7030–7033, the sole examples of the railroad's attempt at rebuilding U25Bs through remanufacturer Morrison-Knudsen, pass through the Mormon Rocks on March 18, 1978, wearing their experimental DAYLIGHT-colored liveries. *Dick Stephenson* Below: A westbound UP freight approaches Highway 138 on November 19, 1977. On the point are three SD40-2s (two in the former 8000-class) and a Southern Pacific SD45T-2 "tunnel motor." *Allan Styffe*

Above: A long westbound Santa Fe freight descends the 3 percent grade on the south track between Gish and Pine Lodge in April 1989 with "Kodachrome" C30-7 8055 on the point. *Elrond G. Lawrence* Below: Santa Fe 5509 East heads upgrade near Alray in February 1971. Santa Fe's pre-"yellowbonnet" colors of the 1960s and 1970s are well illustrated by this SD45/GP35/GP30/SD45 power consist. *Bob Kern*

Above: Number 103, the westbound CITY OF LOS ANGELES, glides between Gish and Pine Lodge in November 1968. The last car is a baggage-dormitory car equipped with a steam generator to supply train heat. The light-colored car near the end of the train is a private car owned by the Las Vegas Press Club. *Leon Callaway* Left: A long AT&SF freight forms a giant ''z'' as it snakes around the curves approaching Alray in October 1974. *Leon Callaway*

Opposite top: Santa Fe 4-4-2 1468 is seen helping 4-8-2 3748 with an eastbound passenger train of heavyweight cars between Pine Lodge and Alray, circa 1940. *Thomas Hotchkiss (Author's Collection)* Opposite below: Southern Pacific and AT&SF trains pass each other at Alray in the 1970s after the Santa Fe had installed CTC on the First District and trains could run either way on either track. The bridges spanned the main highway before the present I-15 freeway was built. *Richard Steinheimer*

1468

SOUTHERN
PACIFIC
SOUTHERN
PACIFIC
6900
Santa Fe
Santa Fe
Santa Fe
Santa Fe

Above: An eastbound SP train descends the grade alongside the Mormon Rocks in June 1979, with two borrowed UP SD40-2s leading two SP units. *Leon Callaway* Below: Santa Fe's eastbound 881 train passes Alray on October 3, 1987, with some unique power—lead unit 5865 is a rebuilt SD45-2, while sister rebuild 5855 has been outfitted with a new Caterpillar prime mover. Trailing unit 7200, now called an SF30-B, is Santa Fe's sole attempt at rebuilding U23Bs. A dynamometer car behind the power records the trio's assault of "the hill." *Elrond G. Lawrence*

Above: In this winter scene taken on February 25, 1987, a westbound UP freight passes above the old main highway (now a fire road) just below where the west switch to Gish siding used to be. The well-digging rig at the right was digging a 12,000-foot hole to study earthquake fault behavior in a government-sponsored project called ''Deep Observation and Sampling of Earth's Continental Crust'' (DOSECC), but funding ran out before the depth was reached and the rig was subsequently removed. *David R. Busse* Below: The floor of the abandoned section gang's living quarters at Alray provides a nice spot for watching trains on a summer afternoon in 1950. The Alco-powered train is the eastbound CHIEF. *Jack Whitmeyer*

Opposite top: An eastbound Union Pacific passenger train with three Fairbanks-Morse units and a steam helper is seen following a UP freight between Cajon creek and Alray in the 1950s. The freight will no doubt take the siding at Alray to let the "varnish" by. *Stan Kistler* Opposite below: Five SD24s, the last three of which are cabless booster units, with an eastbound piggyback freight at Alray in 1966. *Thomas Hotchkiss (Author's Collection)* Above: Santa Fe 4-6-2 type 1372 helping 4-8-2 type 3736 with a train of heavyweight Pullmans below Alray, circa 1940. *Thomas Hotchkiss (Author's Collection)*

Number 210 (Union Pacific No. 10, the CITY OF ST. LOUIS) at Alray about 1960. *C.W. McLaughlin*

Top: Both tunnels are visible in this unusual view taken from the lead unit of a westbound AT&SF freight descending the north track. The lower tunnel is seen through the window in the cab door at the right, while the upper tunnel is visible in the rear-view mirror at left. It's April 22, 1984. *Mike Lepker* Below: The eastbound CHIEF enters the lower tunnel in March 1950. The track in the center is the Alray siding. *Chard L. Walker*

Train No. 116, UP's CITY OF LAS VEGAS, emerges from the upper tunnel on August 16, 1964. *Chard L. Walker*

Opposite above: An eastbound Santa Fe special, headed by FP45 5942 works its way up the Pass at tunnel 2 on the north track in 1976. Santa Fe has long favored the cowl units for passenger specials, using them singly or in sets of up to four. They survive today as the 90-class Super Fleet units. *Steve Patterson (Dick Stephenson Collection)*

Below: Santa Fe No. 17, the westbound SUPER CHIEF, presents a perfect streamliner image at Gish in 1951. Part of the Gish siding is visible beyond the train. *Robert Hale* Left: Santa Fe's NAVAJO with 4-8-4 3754 emerging from one of the tunnels east of Alray in January 1940. *Allan Youell* Opposite below: An F45 and three SD45s lead an eastbound Santa Fe train of COFC and TOFC (Containers and Trailers on Flat Cars) coming through the north track upper tunnel in January 1975. *Hank Graham*

Santa Fe
Santa Fe
Santa Fe
ROCK ISLAND

UNION PACIFIC
403

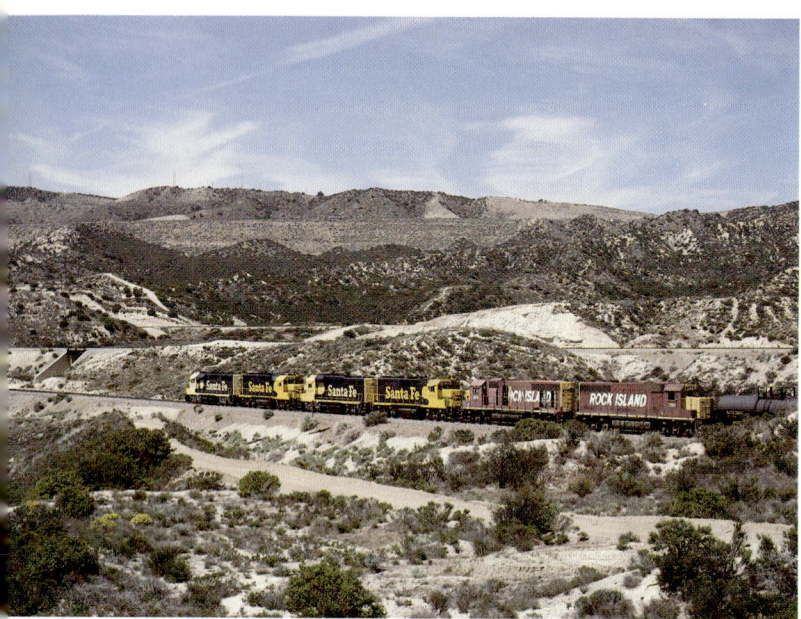

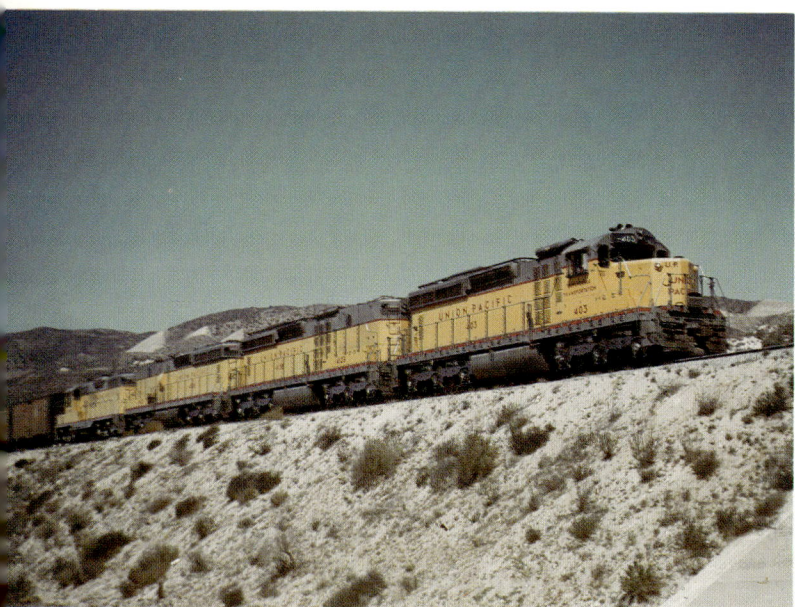

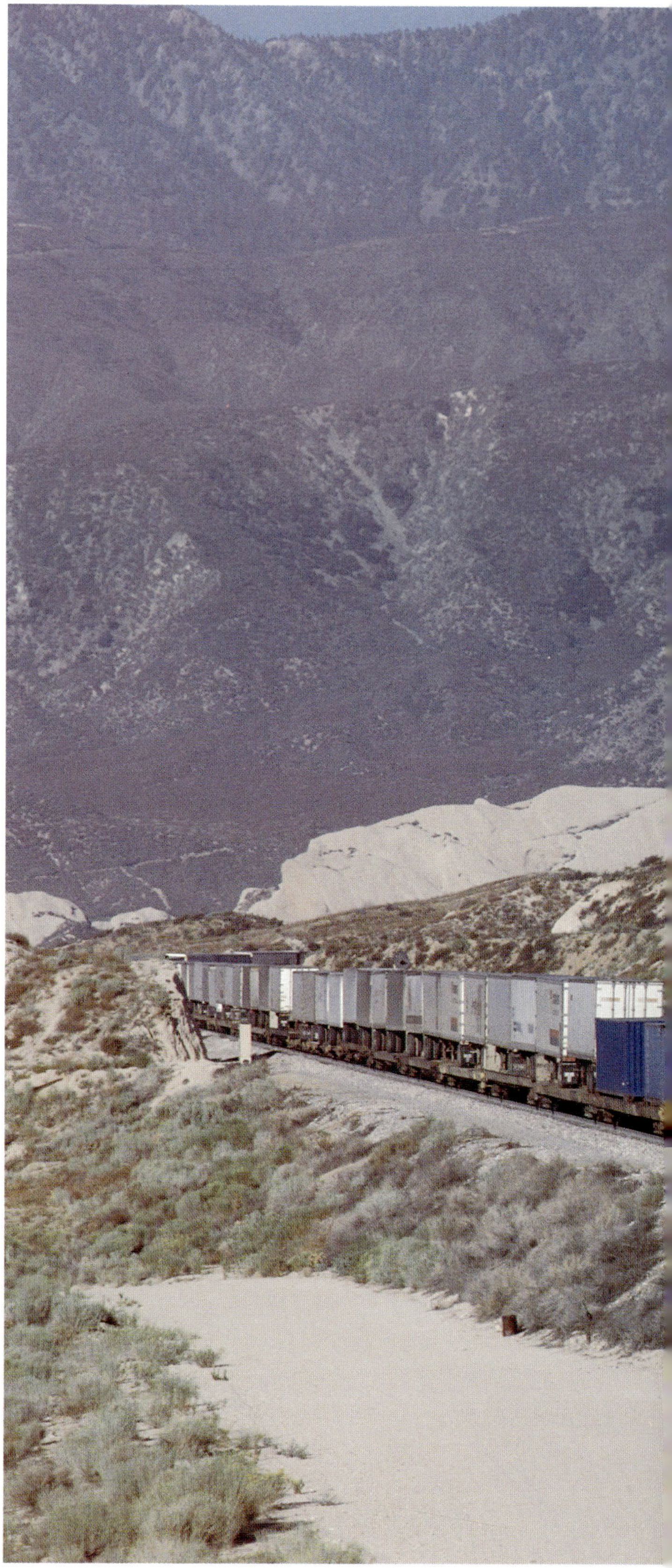

Above Left: This westbound Santa Fe train on the south track a mile west of Summit has two dead-in-consist Rock Island GP40s, 383 and 396, on their way to Chrome Locomotive Co. in San Bernardino, and a date with the scrapper's torch. *Mike Lepker* Below Left: UP SD24 403 leads two SD24 boosters and a GP20 up the hill near Summit as they head east on April 1, 1961. *Allan Styffe* Above: In this nice telephoto view taken August 23, 1985, we see an eastbound Union Pacific train ascending the grade between the Alray tunnels and Summit while a Southern Pacific train is visible to the right. *David R. Busse*

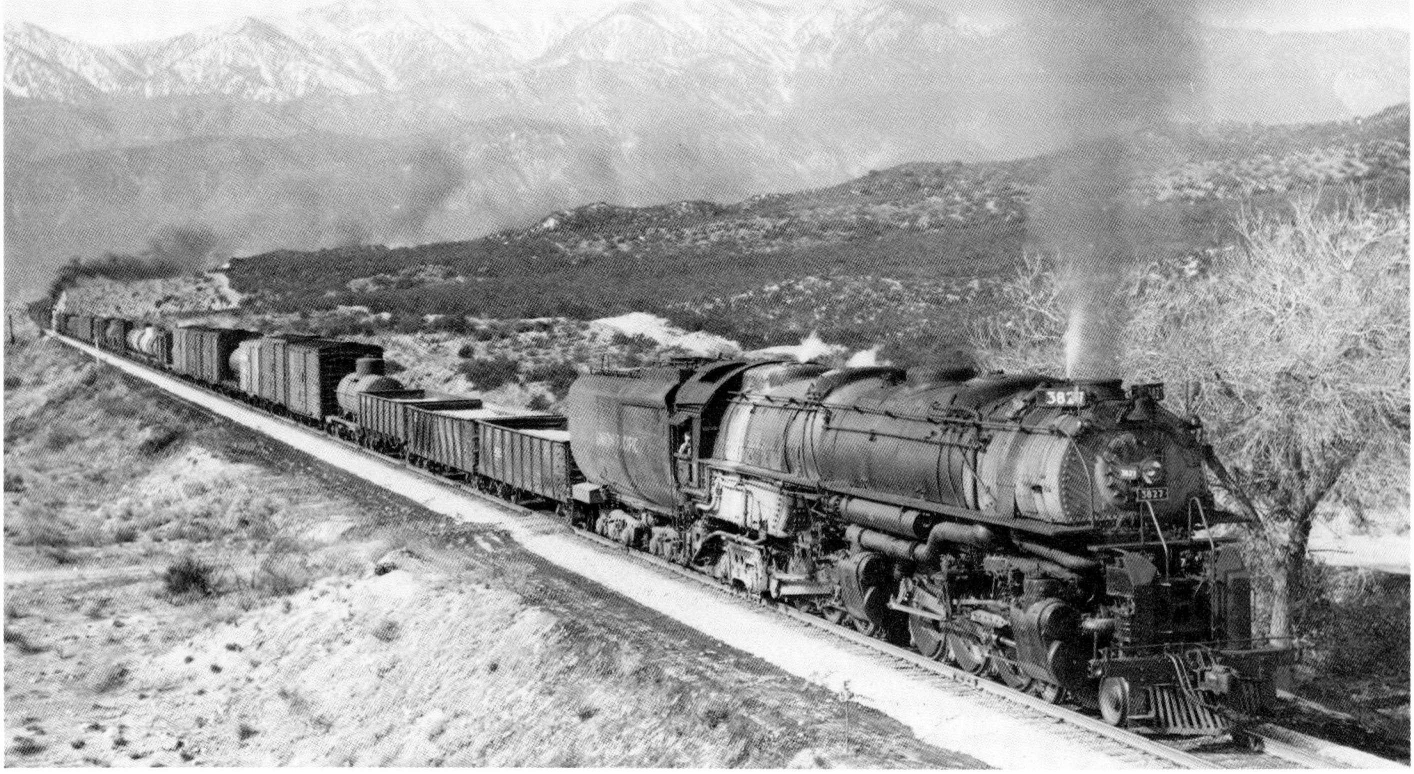
3827

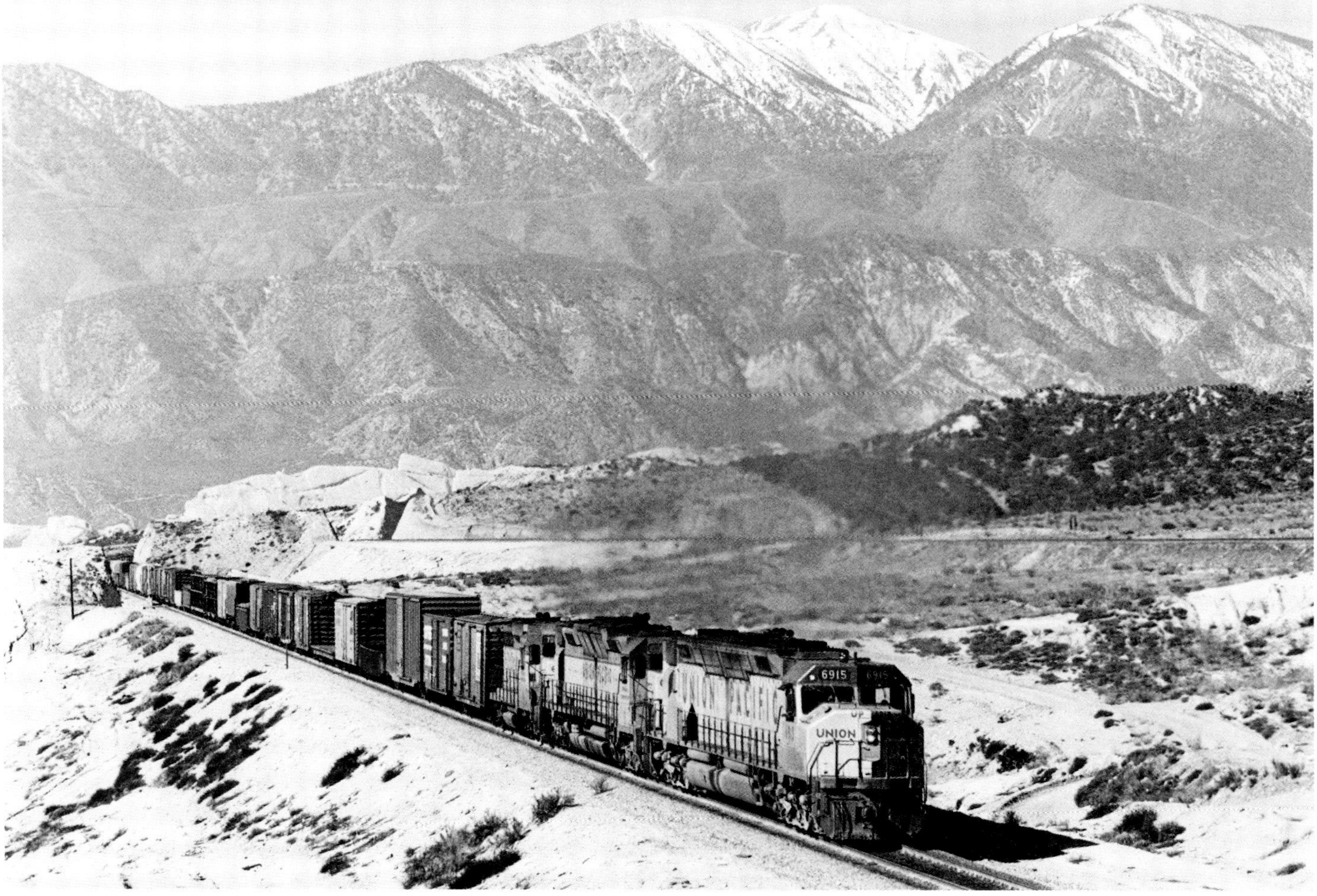
6915
UNION

Opposite top: Union Pacific 4-6-6-4 3827, with engineer Lloyd Porter at the throttle, blasts up the grade past Milepost 58x in February 1947, while two steam helpers shove on the rear ahead of the caboose. *Walt Thrall (John Shaw Collection)* Opposite below: An eastbound Union Pacific freight powered by DDA40X 6915, DD35 71 and GP30 704 climbs the hill at Milepost 58x in March 1972. Above the units is the Southern Pacific line, and above everything else is "Old Baldy" (Mt. San Antonio), the highest peak in the San Gabriel range, at an elevation of 10,080. *Thomas Hotchkiss (Author's Collection)* Below: Four FT units assisted by a steam helper move eastbound tonnage up the 2.2 percent grade of the eastward track between Alray and Summit in the late 1940s. *Frank Peterson (Stan Kistler Collection)* Above: On May 21, 1976, Amtrak inaugurated weekend-only service between Los Angeles and Las Vegas and this first run had four E units on the head end. Subsequent runs had Amtrak's newer 500-class SDP40Fs and 200-class F40PHs. The first train is seen here descending the three percent grade of the south track a few miles west of Summit on May 23 on its return trip to Los Angeles. *Steve Patterson*

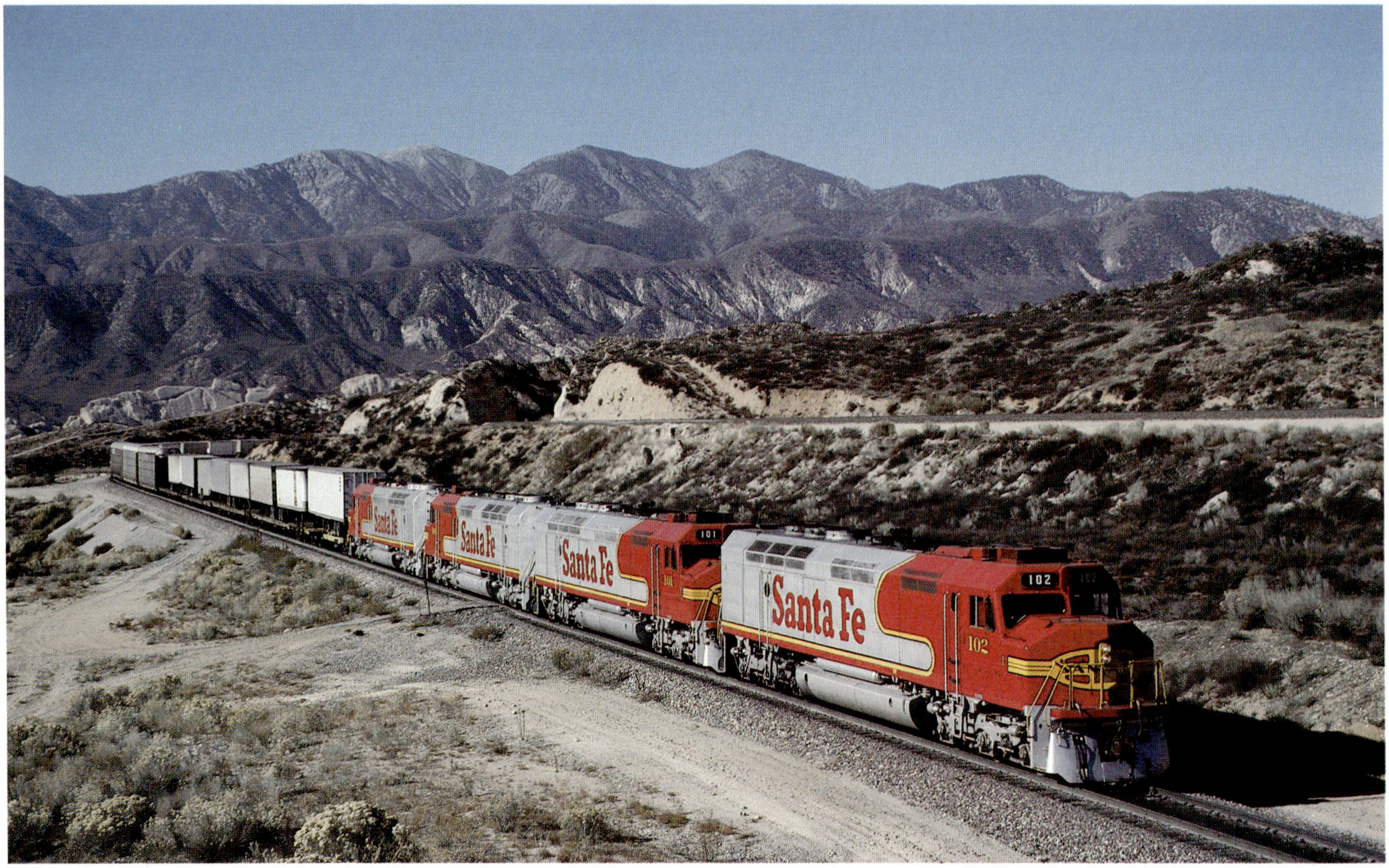
Santa Fe
102

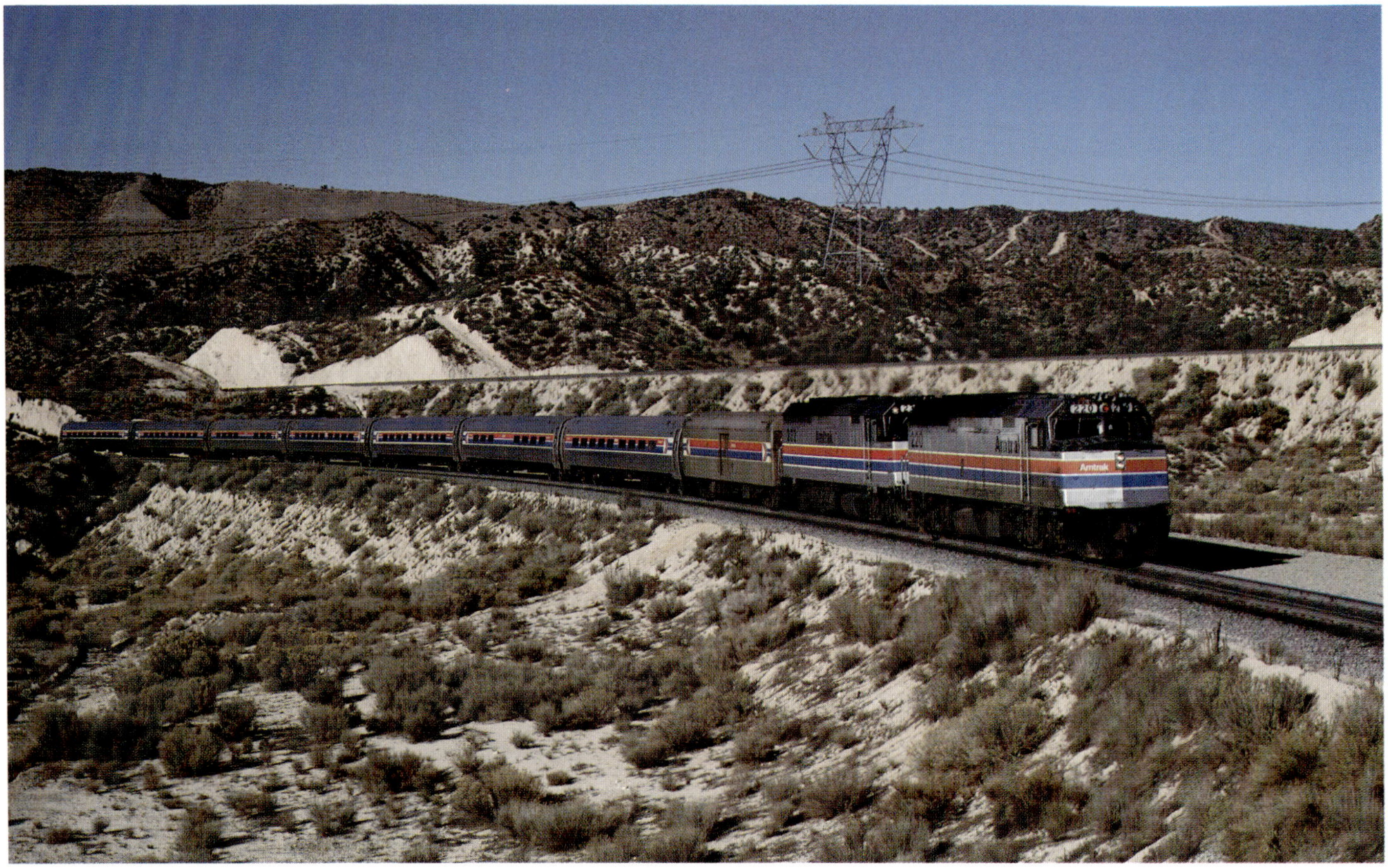
Amtrak

Above Left: On the morning of November 18, 1989, Santa Fe eastbound symbol train 893 sported four Super Fleet SDFP45s, resplendent in their red and silver livery. The train is seen here at MP 58x on the north track a few miles west of Summit; the SP line is visible to the right. *Rod Higbie* Below Left: Amtrak train No. 36, the eastbound DESERT WIND, approaches Milepost 57x on December 29, 1979. Two F40PHs are leading a string of new Amfleet equipment in this view, as they head for Cajon Summit. *Dick Stephenson* Top: UP train No. 2, the eastbound LOS ANGELES LIMITED, has three Fairbanks-Morse road units plus an EMD "cow and calf" helper on September 6, 1952. The train is about one mile west of Summit. *Jack Whitmeyer* Bottom: In 1979, Santa Fe leased a number of locomotives from the Chessie System and Norfolk & Western railroads. This assorted mix of power was seen west of Summit on September 10, 1979. The units consist of Santa Fe SD40-2 5040, N&W SD40-2 6151, B&O GP40s 3710 (in Chessie colors) and 3685, and AT&SF U36C 8771. How's that for variety? *Mike Lepker*

Top: Santa Fe 3934, a 2-10-2 type, on the head end of an eastbound freight below Summit during the spud rush circa 1950. *Thomas Hotchkiss (Author's Collection)* Above: A westbound Southern Pacific freight, led by U28C 7154, climbs the grade just below Hiland in January 1973, while storm clouds gather over the desert. *Thomas Hotchkiss (Author's Collection)*

Top: For America's 1976 bicentennial celebration, Santa Fe painted SD45-2s 5700–5704 in red, white and blue, trimmed with stars and the Great Seal of the United States. The 5700 is on the point of the eastbound SUPER C fast freight at the west end of the 1972 line change, near Milepost 57x on a hazy day. *Santa Fe Railway* Above: Number 203 (Union Pacific Number 3, the westbound UTAHN) heads out of Summit with Alco PA/PB power in the 1950s. *Richard Steinheimer*

9028
9028
MISSOURI PACIFIC
9028
UNION PACIFIC

Amtrak
Amtrak
Amtrak

Top Left: On November 9, 1987, the UP sent a whopping 15-unit power movement east, seen here west of Summit. Missouri Pacific C36-7 9028 is on the point, followed by a second MP unit, 11 UP units, a C&NW SD40-2, and an SP SD45T-2. *Elrond G. Lawrence* Bottom Left: Amtrak's eastbound SUNSET LIMITED, powered by P30CH units 712 and 711, is one and a half miles west of Summit as it detours over the Santa Fe from Colton to Phoenix, Arizona, because of a derailment on the Southern Pacific at Frink, California, near the Salton Sea. The date is July 8, 1989. *Rod Higbie* Top: In 1985 Santa Fe hosted a trio of new EMD SD60 locomotives for testing on AT&SF rails. In this July 13, 1985 photo, the units are seen powering the eastbound 881 train near Milepost 57.5, while an SP eastbound descends the grade in the background. *Mark Denis; Dick Stephenson collection* Bottom: This westbound SP train is heading toward Mojave, and is seen climbing the Cajon grade about a half mile below Hiland on June 26, 1984. Note the articulated doublestack container car behind the units. In the distance, a UP train is visible on the north track, as well as portions of Santa Fe's north and south tracks. *David R. Busse*

Left: Second 24, a section of the eastbound GRAND CANYON LIMITED, led by 4-8-4 3759, passes the west yard limit board beyond the 10-degree curve west of Summit. The train is headed due south by compass direction. Note the phone booth and the crossover between the tracks in this June 1952 photo. *Jack Whitmeyer* Below: Second 23, a section of the westbound GRAND CANYON, with 4-8-4 2929 and mostly heavyweight cars, on the 10-degree curve just west of Summit in the very early 1950s. *Robert Hale*

Opposite: The safety valve lifts on 4-8-4 2923 as the engineer closes the throttle. First 24 is rounding the long curve coming into Summit on a cloudy day in the early 1950s. *Robert Hale*

Top: In February 1989, Santa Fe produced a promotional film entitled *The Quality Way,* to showcase the railway's latest equipment and services. As part of the filming, AT&SF borrowed F-units 347C and 347B from the California State Railroad Museum in Sacramento, and used several cars from its private passenger car fleet to simulate the railway's classic SUPER CHIEF passenger train. Since the F-units are not operational, an SD40-2/GP40X duo was placed at the rear of the train to push it during filming sequences. The train is seen here on the north track on the "big curve" just west of Summit. At the upper right can be seen a bit of the old grade used prior to the 1972 line change—technically no CHIEF ever operated through *this* curve. *Elrond G. Lawrence* Lit by the last rays of the setting sun, an eastbound Santa Fe passenger train heads toward Summit on a snowy January 8, 1955 day. *Ray Ballash*

Above: In this late afternoon view of a westbound UP train west of Summit, the moon can be seen above lead SD40-2 3762. The date is August 16, 1986. *David R. Busse* Below: Two zebra-striped GP9s with an eastbound cab-hop enter the curve into Summit on October 8, 1960. *Allan Styffe*

Santa Fe No. 22, the eastbound EL CAPITAN, snakes through the curves west of Summit, circa 1952. Just behind the last car is the phone booth and crossover. Both were removed soon afterward. *Robert Hale*

Top: UP GP7 130 is on the point of a unique train on this January 6, 1957 day—it's leading UP train No. 116, the CITY OF LAS VEGAS, which, for a nine-month period in 1956–1957, consisted of General Motors' AEROTRAIN. It's seen heading into the "big curve" west of Summit. Bottom: Santa Fe F7A 287C is seen leading a "mixed bag" of Geeps and F-units out of Summit on April 1, 1961. *Two photos, Allan Styffe*

Top: A glistening EL CAPITAN rolls past the "train" sign at Summit on March 31, 1956. *Ray Ballash* Bottom: A quartet of F7s is on the point of Santa Fe Extra 278C West as it departs Summit on January 6, 1957. The Summit wye can be seen at right. *Allan Styffe*

Right: A westbound Union Pacific freight with engine 5024 (2-10-2) pulls through the cut at the west end of Summit in November 1941. *Frank Peterson (Bob Kern Collection)*

An eastbound AT&SF freight with ''alligator'' Alco RSD15 on the point nears Summit in the 1960s. *Henry Brueckman*

Top: Activity at the west end of the Summit yard on June 6, 1948: a westbound Union Pacific passenger train with 4-8-2 7853 on the point rolls by while a westbound UP freight with EMD carbody units waits in the westward siding. A UP 1360-class Fairbanks-Morse helper waits on the west end of the westward siding (center), while Santa Fe 2-10-2 helper 3895 waits on the west leg of the wye at right. Another Santa Fe helper waits on the eastward siding (above the 7853's front end). *Lewis Harris* Above: Activity at Summit in 1952: at left, an eastbound AT&SF freight arrives with a two-unit FT helper, a westbound AT&SF waits in the westward siding with FT 151 wearing an unusual short-lived paint scheme and UP cow-and-calf helper 1870 is on the west leg of the wye. The Summit post office is the light-colored building in the middle distance, just to the right of the second pole from right. *Stan Kistler*

Top: Red and silver F7A 305 leads an eastbound passenger train into Summit in June 1966. *Bob Kern* Bottom: UP 8073, an SD40-2, leads a pair of DDA40X Centennials into Summit on March 31, 1979. *Allan Styffe*

Top: A pair of Centennials, led by DDA40X 6944, pulls a westbound drag out of Summit, as the train begins its descent of the grade into the west side of Cajon on March 16, 1972. Bottom: A snow-covered Cajon is the scene for this view of Extra 1878 West, as it pulls out of Summit on March 5, 1970. *Two photos, Allan Styffe*

One day in the spring of 1971, an eastbound Union Pacific railfan special with E9A 909 on the point passed No. 103, the westbound CITY OF LOS ANGELES, led by E-unit 952 just west of Summit. Both ends of both trains passed each other at the same spot. UP business car 111 brought up the markers of No. 103. *Both Photos, Leon Callaway*

A westbound AT&SF freight powered by 2-10-2 3856 leaves Summit back in August 1939. The top of the old passenger car used for a depot can be seen to the right of the trees above the train. *Walt Thrall (John Shaw Collection)*

Union Pacific 3631, a 2-8-8-0, entering the westward main from the west leg of the wye at Summit in November 1936. At the upper right, another helper is about to back down the east leg of the wye. *Alton Parsons*

A spectacular snowscape at Summit: Santa Fe Extra 5366 East emerges from the "new" cut in December of 1987, as the San Gabriel Mountains provide a majestic backdrop.
John Sistrunk

HESPERIA ·

Top: An eastbound Santa Fe freight led by engine 3939 comes into Summit in June 1940. *Walt Thrall (John Shaw Collection)* Above: Railfans photograph the rear of No. 20, the eastbound CHIEF, on June 14, 1952, while a Union Pacific cow-and-calf helper waits on the engine track and AT&SF 2-10-2 3878 sits on the eastward siding. *Jack Whitmeyer*

Below: Union Pacific 3823, a 4-6-6-4, powers an eastbound freight past Summit in 1947. Note the brakeman standing on the army truck on the second flatcar. *Malcolm Gaddis* Above: An early diesel pulls the westbound Union Pacific LOS ANGELES LIMITED past the old Los Angeles Railway's funeral streetcar DESCANSO and Summit depot in March 1947. *Chard L. Walker*

Above: Santa Fe PA 71, leading a quintet of the classy Alcos, passes the Summit depot in July 1966, leading a westbound mail train. *Bob Kern*
Above Right: Santa Fe Extra 3879 East passes the Summit depot on May 29, 1950. *Chard L. Walker* Below Right: It's July 9, 1951, and Santa Fe train No. 24, the eastbound GRAND CANYON LIMITED, is ready to continue on its way after cutting helper 3151 off. The 3151 was a 2-8-2 Mikado, and 3776 a 4-8-4 Northern. *Chard L. Walker*

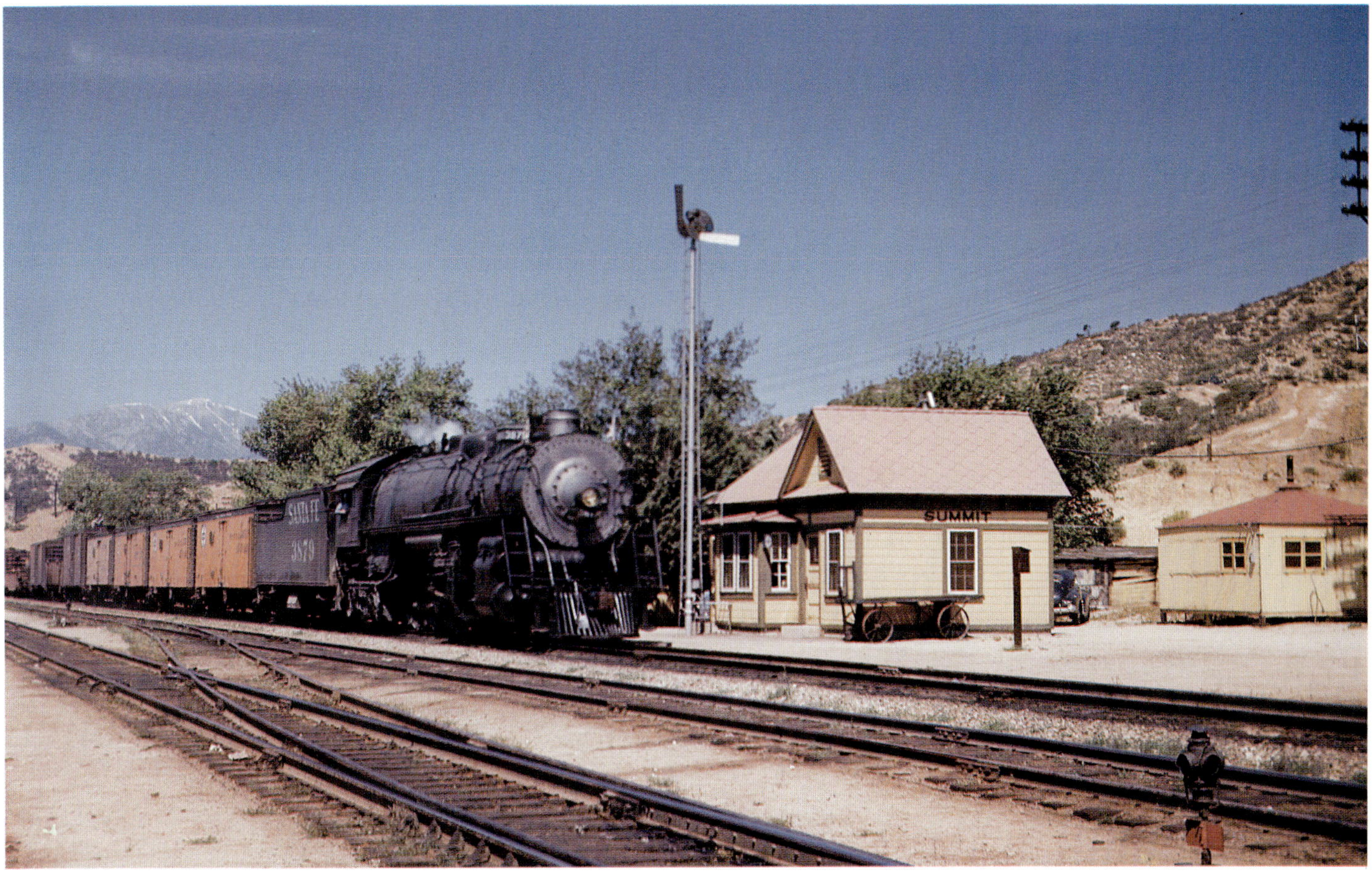
SANTA FE
3879
SUMMIT

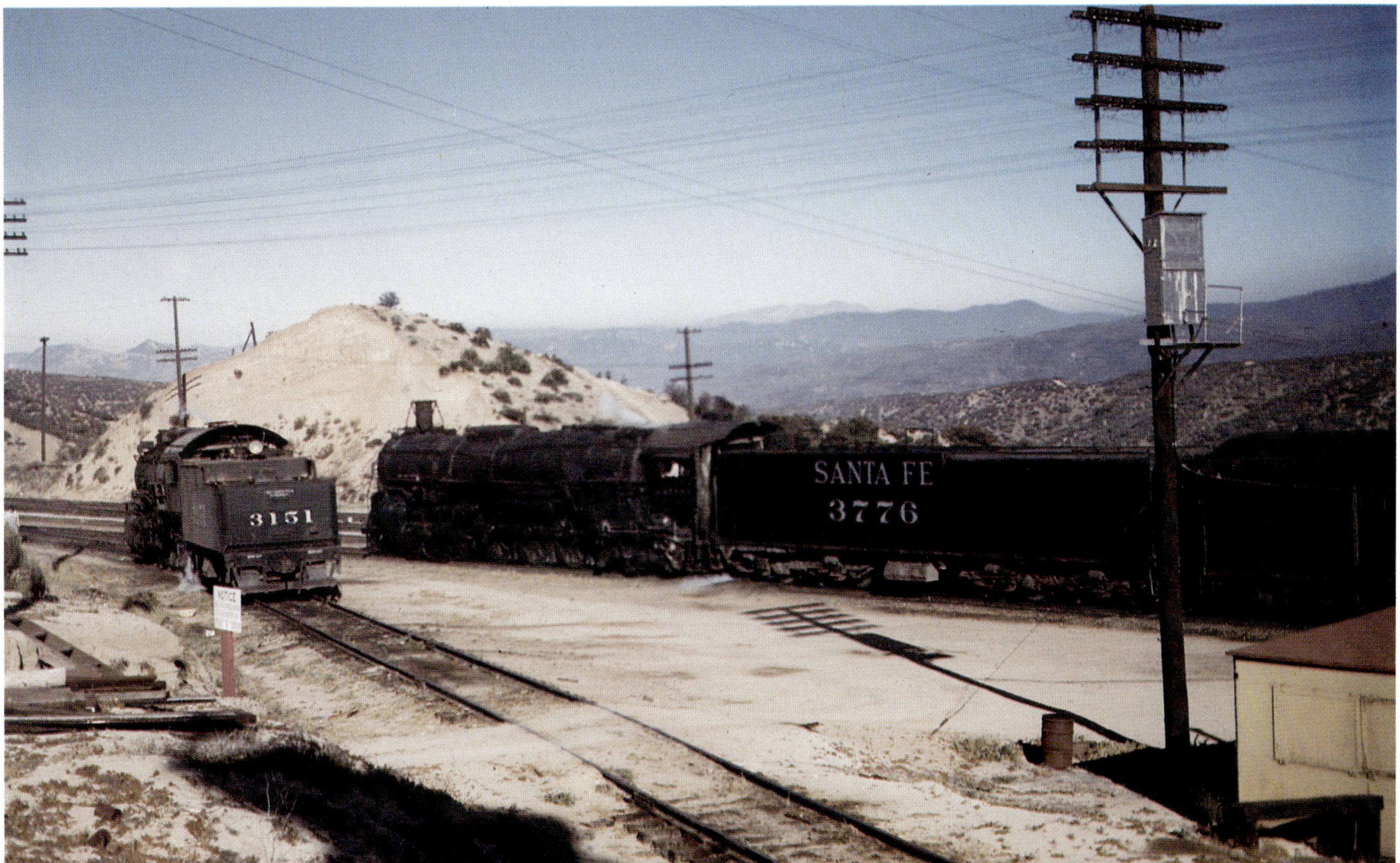
3151
SANTA FE
3776

Top: Union Pacific's CITY OF ST. LOUIS is westbound at Summit, passing a railfan special run by the Orange Empire Trolley Museum (now the Orange Empire Railway Museum) on January 28, 1967, to observe construction on the new Southern Pacific line. The PA-powered special sits in the westbound siding. *Elmer K. Hall (Dick Stephenson Collection)*

Above: The Union Pacific used the General Motors Aerotrain on Nos. 115 and 116, the CITY OF LAS VEGAS trains, for a time. The train required a helper from San Bernardino to Summit, in the form of a UP GP9. This photo was taken on February 3, 1957, at Summit, just after helper 294 had cut off and backed into the engine track. A trace of snow remains here and there. *John Shaw*

Top: Two 2800-class Fairbanks-Morse units help a 3800-class 2-10-2 with a westbound freight into Summit in 1952. The 2800 series was soon renumbered into the 3000 series. *Stan Kistler* Above: Activity at Summit on June 14, 1952: Union Pacific's eastbound LOS ANGELES LIMITED is leaving after cutting off the cow-and-calf helper seen on the engine track at right. Behind it is a three-unit Santa Fe helper in zebra stripes. To the left of the passenger train are two 3800-class Santa Fe 2-10-2 helpers. Just beyond the east leg of the wye (at far left) is the domestic water car on the stock track, and beyond it is the stock pen. The autos parked near the depot belong to visiting railfans. *Robert Hale*

Top: Santa Fe 271 East passes the Summit depot on January 4, 1961. Ten units are in charge of this train today, consisting of six F-units and four Geeps. *Allan Styffe* Bottom: Extra 212 West arrives at Summit with helper 3841 on the point. The date is June 7, 1952, the last year that Santa Fe used steam power on freights and helpers during the annual "spud rush." The 3841 was a 2-10-2 (Santa Fe type). *Jack Whitmeyer* Top Right: A quiet scene at Summit, as GP9 711 switches out water cars behind the Summit depot in December 1966. *Bob Kern* Bottom Right: Southern Pacific train No. 807, a third-class westbound freight with SD9 3945 on the point, passes through Hiland on September 29, 1967. Santa Fe's Summit depot had been closed several months earlier that year, and the train order semaphore already removed. *Chard L. Walker*

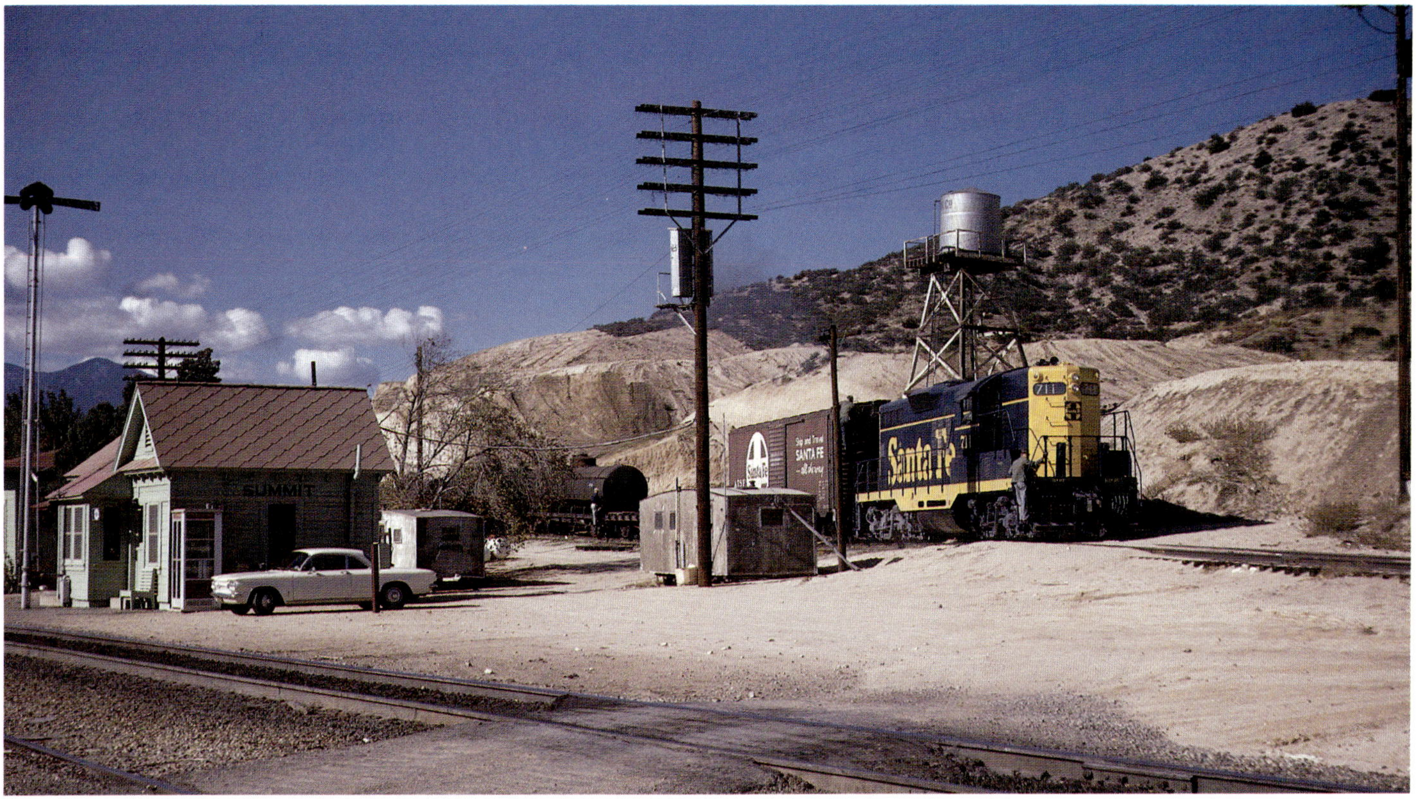
SUMMIT
Santa Fe
711

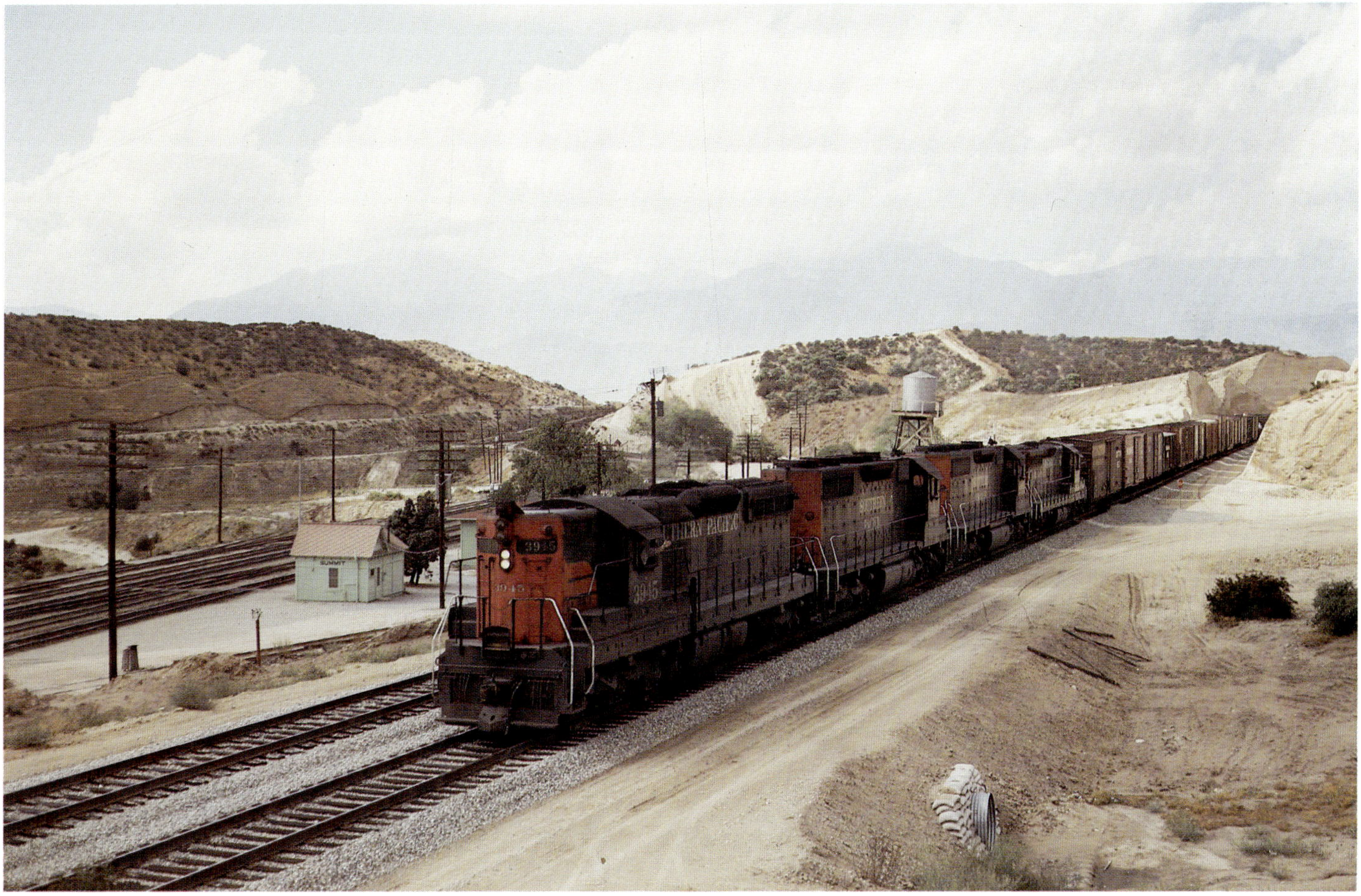
3945

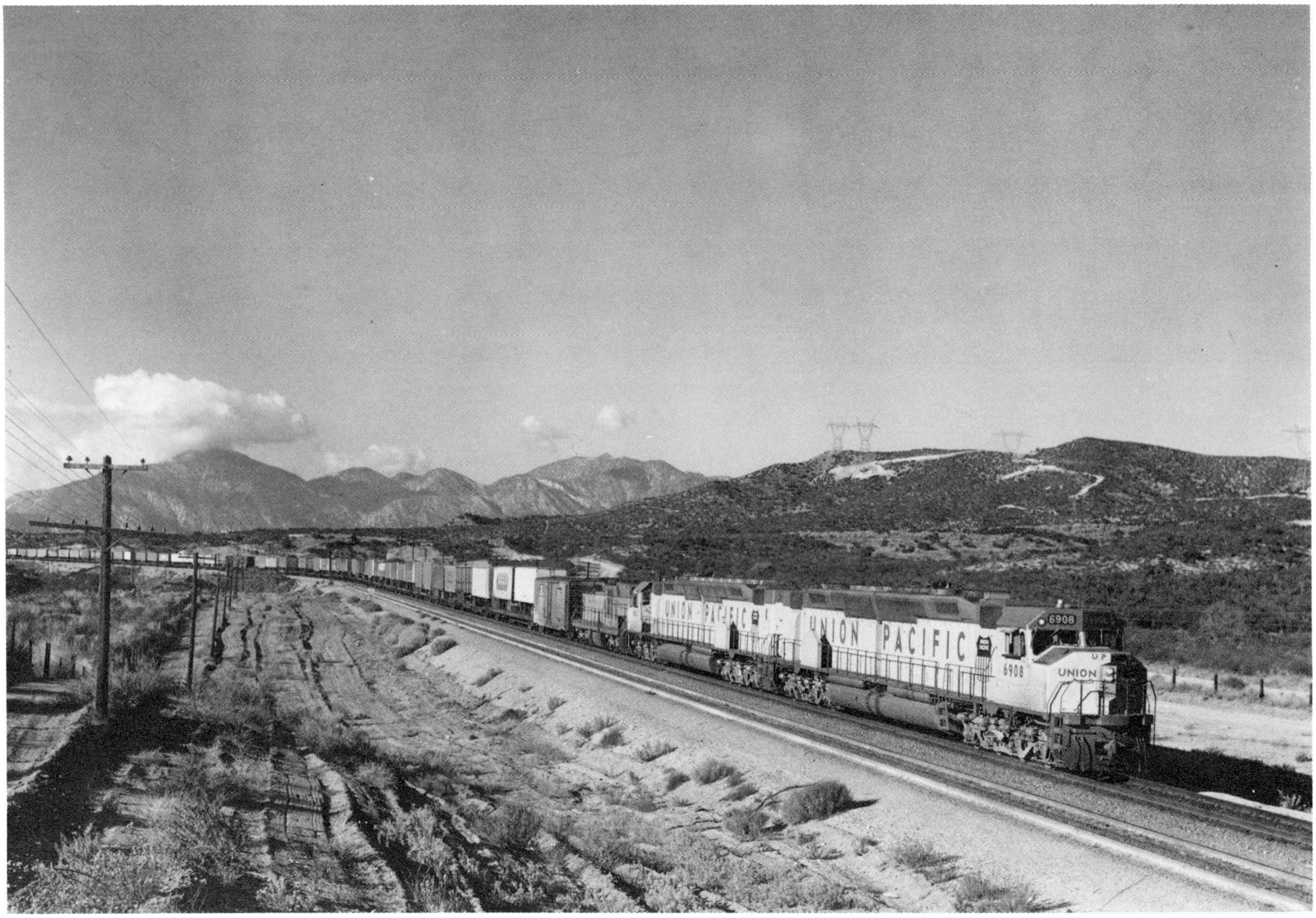
UNION PACIFIC
6908
UNION

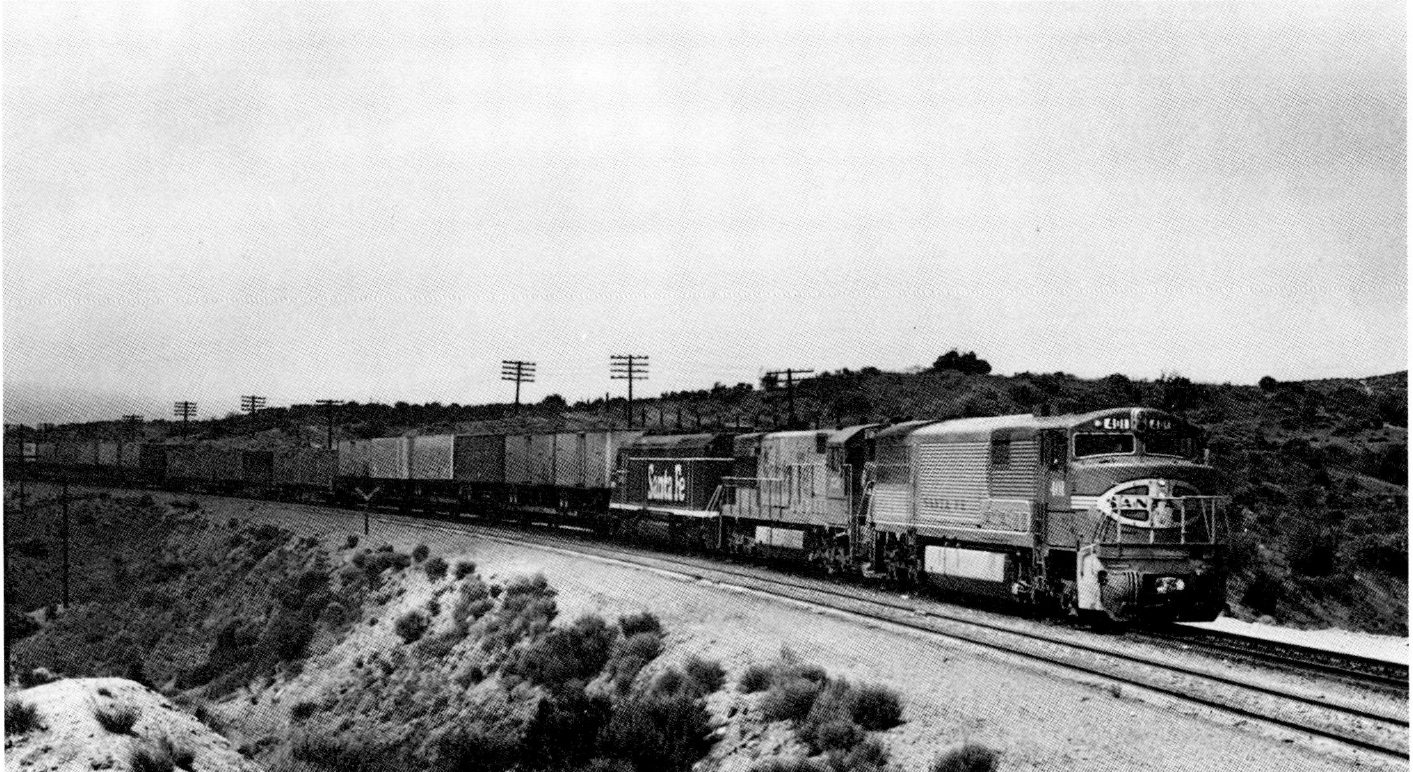
Santa Fe

Opposite top: Two Centennial units and a cabless SD24 lead an eastbound freight east of Summit in the early 1970s. Opposite below: The eastbound Santa Fe SUPER C passes the Y-shaped yard limit sign east of Summit on a cloudy day in the spring of 1967. GE U30CG 401 is on the point, followed by a U28CG and an EMD F45. The GE units were not used this far west on the Santa Fe very often. *Both Photos, Thomas Hotchkiss (Author's Collection)*

Number 201 (Union Pacific No. 1, the westbound LOS ANGELES LIMITED) with UP's first three-unit set of Fairbanks-Morse passenger units, is about one-quarter mile east of the Summit depot on April 4, 1947. *Chard L. Walker*

Below: A westbound Union Pacific passenger train climbs the grade between Lugo and Summit in the 1940s. Helper 5094, a 4-10-2, and road engine 7850, a 4-8-2, combine their efforts to produce a dramatic picture. *Thomas Hotchkiss (Author's Collection)*

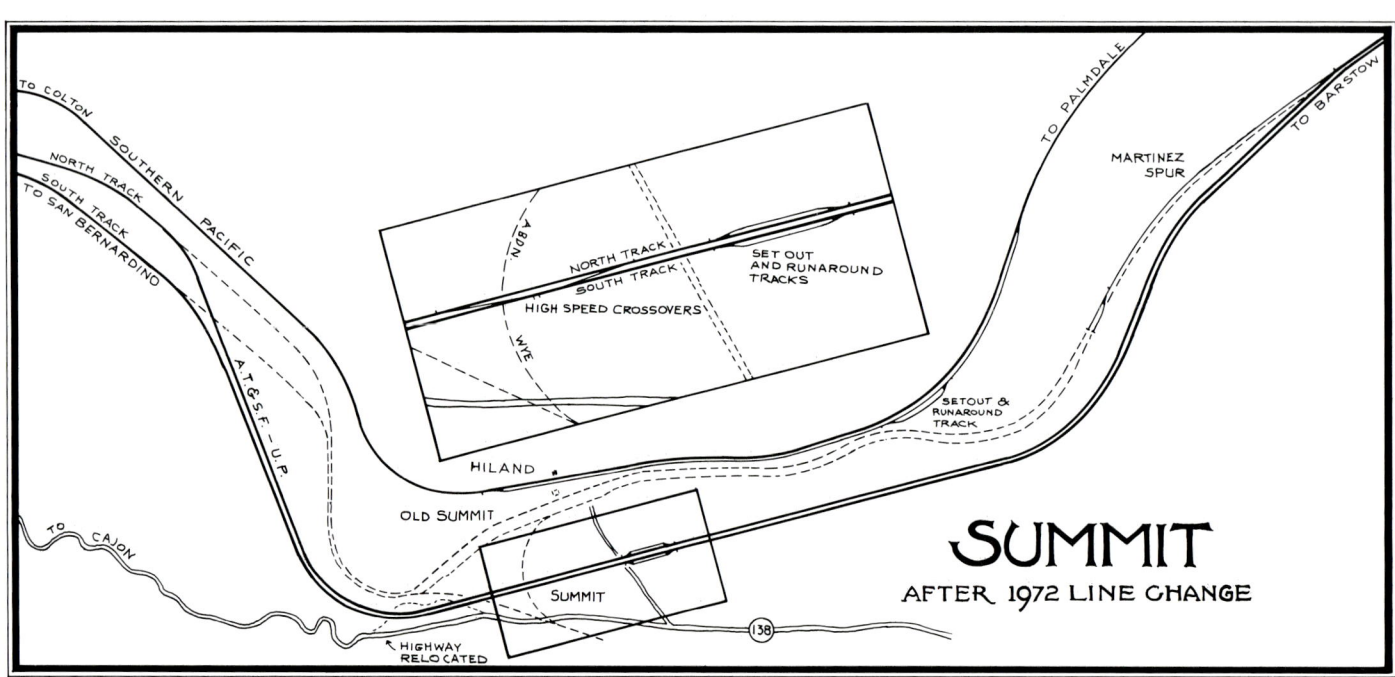

Above: This westbound (heading toward Palmdale) SP train is entering the siding at Hiland on October 3, 1987, and features locomotives from Burlington Northern and Conrail to brighten an otherwise gray consist. *Elrond G. Lawrence* Right: A blanket of snow covers the ground as Santa Fe 3375, a GP35, leads a westbound train through Summit in December 1979. *Russell Eslick; Dick Stephenson collection*

SUMMIT
AFTER 1972 LINE CHANGE

Top: Two Alco RSD15s and two EMD SD24s power a westbound AT&SF freight past signal 541 a half mile east of Summit in 1966. *Thomas Hotchkiss (Author's Collection)* Above left: A westbound Union Pacific freight approaches Summit on November 2, 1941. The road engine is 2-10-2 5518, and the helper is 2-8-2 2264. *Richard H. Kindig* Above right: Union Pacific helper 3560, a 2-8-8-0, runs light near Lugo, en route to Victorville in 1947. *Frank Peterson (Bob Kern Collection)*

Top: AT&SF 4-8-4 2924 heads a westbound passenger train between Lugo and Summit in 1950. *James Ady* Above: SD24 919 leads an eastbound Santa Fe train of empty coal hoppers through Lugo on October 3, 1969. The Lugo siding leads to the lower right corner of the photo, while the track on the far left was the setout spur. *Thomas Hotchkiss (Author's Collection)*

Above: In this time exposure taken in 1963, an eastbound UP freight passes Summit while the planet Jupiter and the full moon rise in the east. The locomotive headlight illuminates a reflectorized yellow speed limit sign to the left of the tracks, and the caboose markers leave behind two red streaks. Moonlight reflects from the tops of the rails. *Chard L. Walker* Below: On June 14, 1952, Santa Fe local freight had 2-8-2 (Mikado-type) engine 3243. It's seen here at Milepost 54, two miles east of Summit. *Jack Whitmeyer* Above Right: UP train No. 103, the westbound CITY OF LOS ANGELES, ascends the grade near MP 54 in November 1969. The new SP line can be seen in upper left. *Chard L. Walker* Below Right: It's January 4, 1961, and a westbound UP train is arriving at Summit after several minutes of climbing the east side of the pass. UP 280 is on the point; trailing are four more of the high-hood units, including a cabless GP9. *Allan Styffe*

PACIFIC
911
UNION PACIFIC

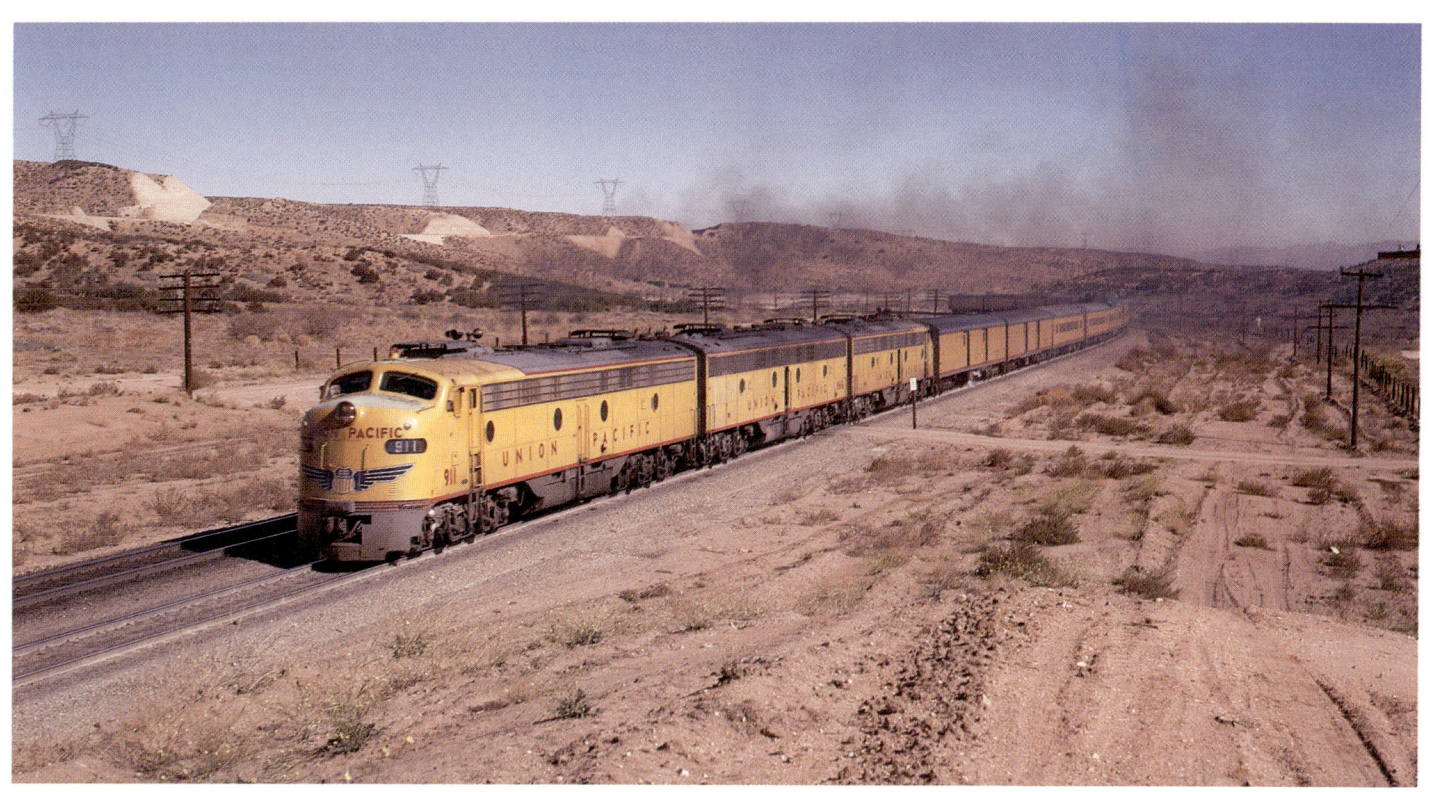

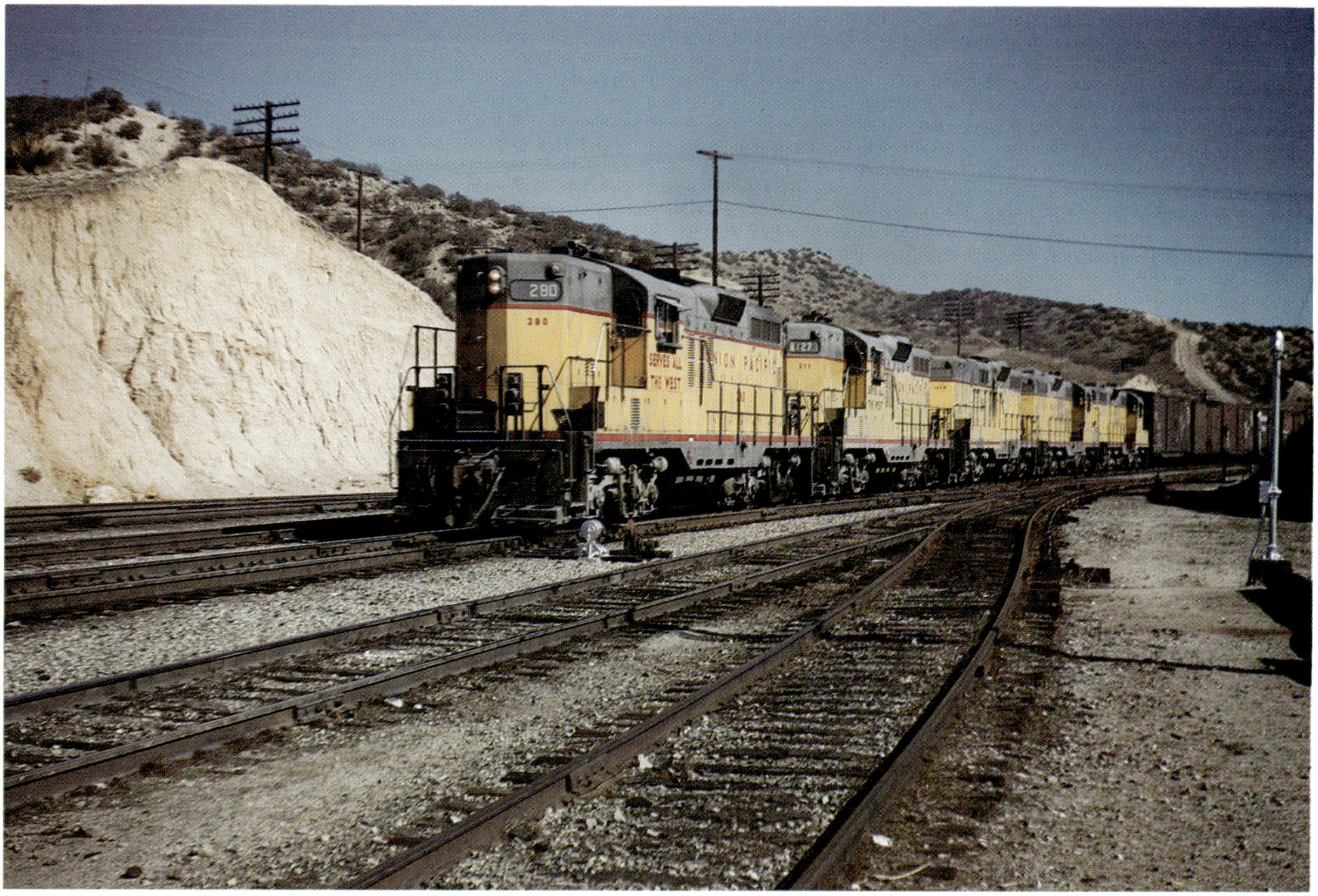
280
SERVES ALL THE WEST
UNION PACIFIC

Top: Union Pacific Challenger 3978, one of the newer 4-6-6-4s rarely seen on Cajon, drifts down the grade at Lugo in 1948 with an eastbound freight drag. *Frank Peterson (Bob Kern Collection)* Above: A westbound Santa Fe freight at the east end of Lugo in May 1949. The phone booth was typical, and every blind siding had one at the time. *Frank Peterson (Bob Kern Collection)*

Left: A section of the westbound GRAND CANYON with 4-8-4 2907 in command passes the heading-in switch to the westward siding at Summit in the early 1950s. *Robert Hale* Above: In June 1948, the Southern Pacific leased several UP 4-6-6-4s to help ease a motive power shortage during the busy season. Since the UP had already dieselized its freight power west of Salt Lake City, the locomotives had to come all the way from Utah, working their way on westbound freight trains. Pictured here are the 3816 and 3817 at the east end of Summit siding on June 15. *James Ady*

A trio of Southern Pacific bicentennial units, consisting of GP40P-2 3197, SD45T-2 9389, and U25BE 6800, lead a westbound (by timetable direction) train through Hiland Siding in January 1976. *Don Jocelyn; Dick Stephenson Collection*

Top: An eastbound Southern Pacific train led by Cotton Belt (St. Louis Southwestern) SD45T-2 9266 is passing the west switch to the siding at Hiland on August 11, 1973, on its way to West Colton. *John Shaw* Above: This November 1980 scene shows a westbound Santa Fe train on the south track of the new (1972) line near the east end of the three-mile line change. A 3,780-foot portion of the old eastward track was left intact to be used for storing cars. It's now known as Martinez Spur (named for the roadmaster in charge during the line change). Several cars can be seen on the spur at the far left. In the distance is a bit of the Southern Pacific line, which abruptly disappears into a cut. *Bob Gottier*

Top: Amtrak's SOUTHWEST LIMITED has almost reached the summit of Cajon Pass as it heads west in the early morning with a mixed consist of primarily ex-Santa Fe equipment passing over land that was once part of the Lugo Ranch. In the background is Southern Pacific's Palmdale-Colton Cutoff that soon turns west and heads across the Antelope Valley on its way to Tehachapi. The photo was taken circa 1977–78. *George Manley (Dick Stephenson Collection)*

Above: This eastbound Union Pacific freight is just east of Lugo. Westbound signal 491 is located at the heading-in switch to the siding, above the first unit. This 1966 scene looks up little Antelope Valley toward Summit. *Thomas Hotchkiss (Author's Collection)*

Top: EMD F45 5901 and GE U33C 8501 lead Santa Fe's hotshot SUPER C eastbound at Lugo on February 18, 1971. *Thomas Hotchkiss (Author's Collection)* Above: This eastbound Union Pacific freight at Lugo featured a rather unusual lashup of units: D&RGW SD45 5337, UP U50C 5028 and UP DD35 78. The date is February 24, 1974. *Thomas Hotchkiss (Author's Collection)*

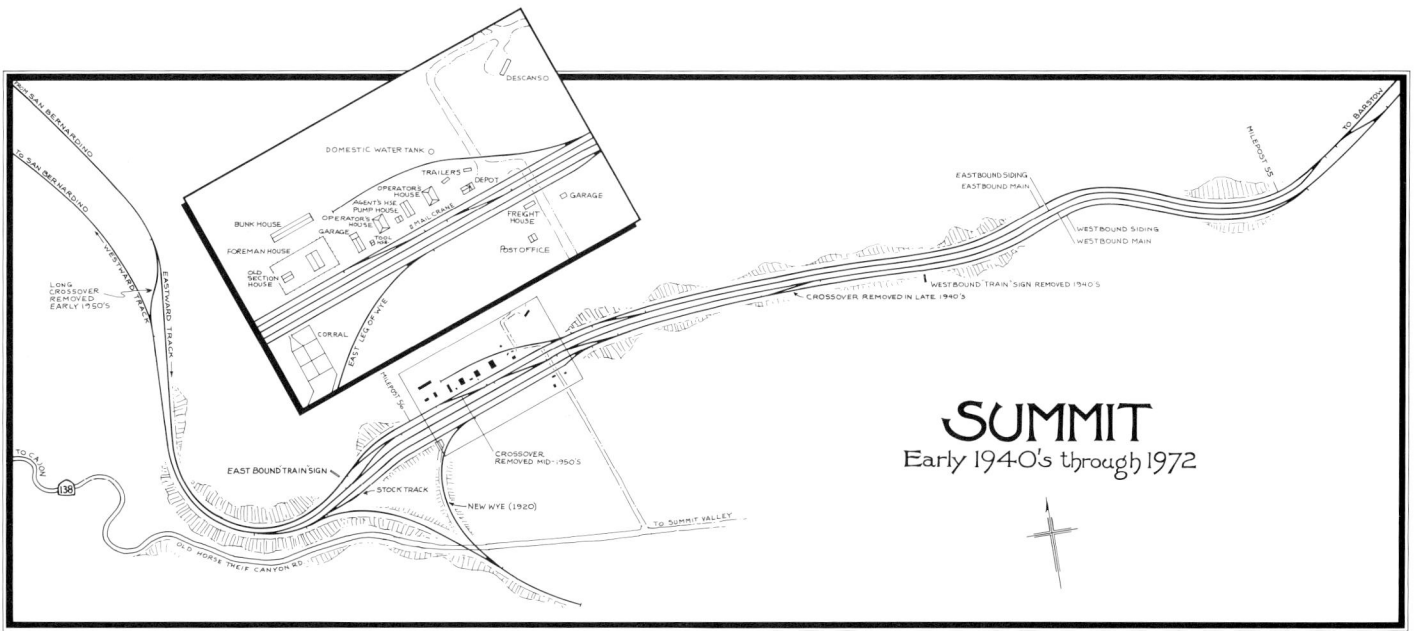

A layer of fog fills Cajon Canyon on the morning of September 25, 1971, but elsewhere a bright sun shines from a cloudless sky in this view of an eastbound Union Pacific freight (led by DDA40X 6935) descending Antelope Valley between Summit and Lugo. *Thomas Hotchkiss (Author's Collection)*

Top: Number 103, the westbound CITY OF LOS ANGELES, is seen here approaching Lugo in the 1960s. Below Lugo the line has fewer curves and more tangent track. *Thomas Hotchkiss (Author's Collection)* Above: Number 210, the eastbound CITY OF ST. LOUIS (No. 10), between Summit and Lugo in 1956. Note the new welded rail on both sides of the eastward track. Soon it will replace the rails that the train is now running on. *Thomas Hotchkiss (Author's Collection)*

Top: A Baltimore and Ohio business car decorates No. 20, the eastbound CHIEF, at Milepost 52 between Summit and Lugo in the 1950s. *Thomas Hotchkiss (Author's Collection)* Above: This westbound Union Pacific freight between Hesperia and Lugo in January 1956 was powered by three GP9 units. The second unit is cabless—a feature that was fairly common on the UP but extremely rare on the Santa Fe. *Thomas Hotchkiss (Author's Collection)*

Above: A westbound AT&SF train is on the north track and a short work train is on the south track a few miles east of Summit in this view taken November 23, 1981. The SP line is quite visible on the hillside. *David R. Busse* Left: For a short time in the late 1960s and early 1970s the Santa Fe ran a short piggyback train between Chicago and Los Angeles known as the SUPER C . . . billed as the ''world's fastest freight train.'' In this view taken on July 1, 1969, the east-bound SUPER C is seen passing Lugo with units 352, 350 and 400. The 350-class units were GE U28CGs, later renumbered into the 7900-class, while the 400-class were U30CGs, later renumbered into the 800-class. *Chard L. Walker*

Top: The hi-levels of Santa Fe's westbound EL CAPITAN bring up the markers as the streamliner passes the east switch of Summit in June 1966. *Bob Kern* Bottom: This westbound SP train is headed for Palmdale on June 14, 1986, when ''SPSF'' merger colors were quite common. The train is between the Hivolt spur and Interstate I-15, near Hesperia. *Arthur Anderson*

Above: A westbound Union Pacific freight with 4-6-6-4 3839 on the point is about to pass UP light helper engine 5090 west of Hesperia in April 1947. *Chard Walker* Left: A westbound Union Pacific mail and passenger train with a 4-8-2 passes under the signal bridge supporting eastward signal 482 and westward signal 481 between Hesperia and Lugo in the mid-1940s. *Thomas Hotchkiss (Author's Collection)* Opposite below: A 2-10-2 helper on the rear of a westbound freight is seen at Milepost 48, between Hesperia and Lugo, circa 1950. *Thomas Hotchkiss (Author's Collection)* Opposite top: Third 23, a section of the westbound GRAND CANYON, at Hesperia in December 1952. This 4-8-4 is now on display at the Museum of Science and Industry in Chicago. *James Ady*

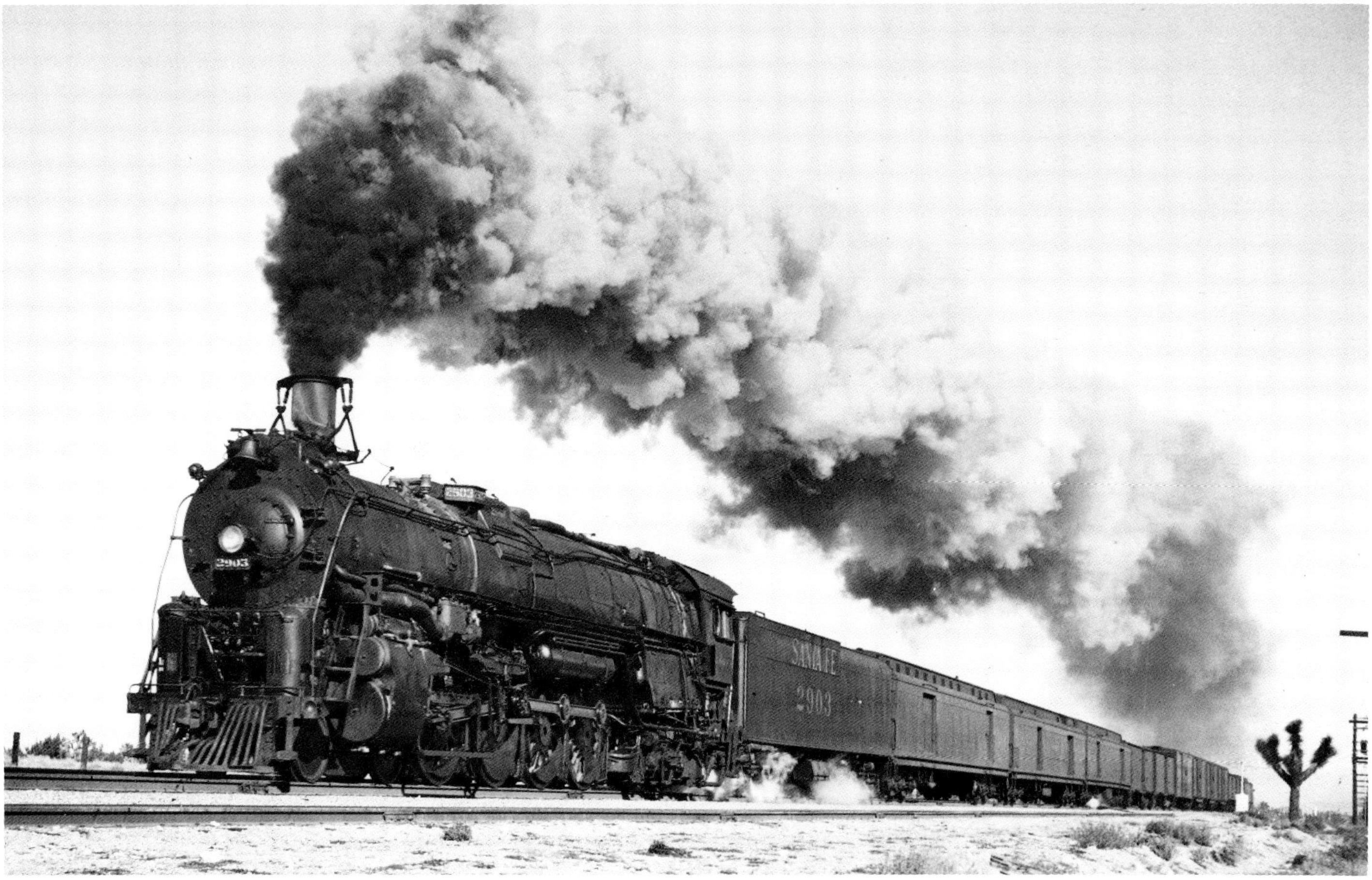
SANTA FE
2903
2903

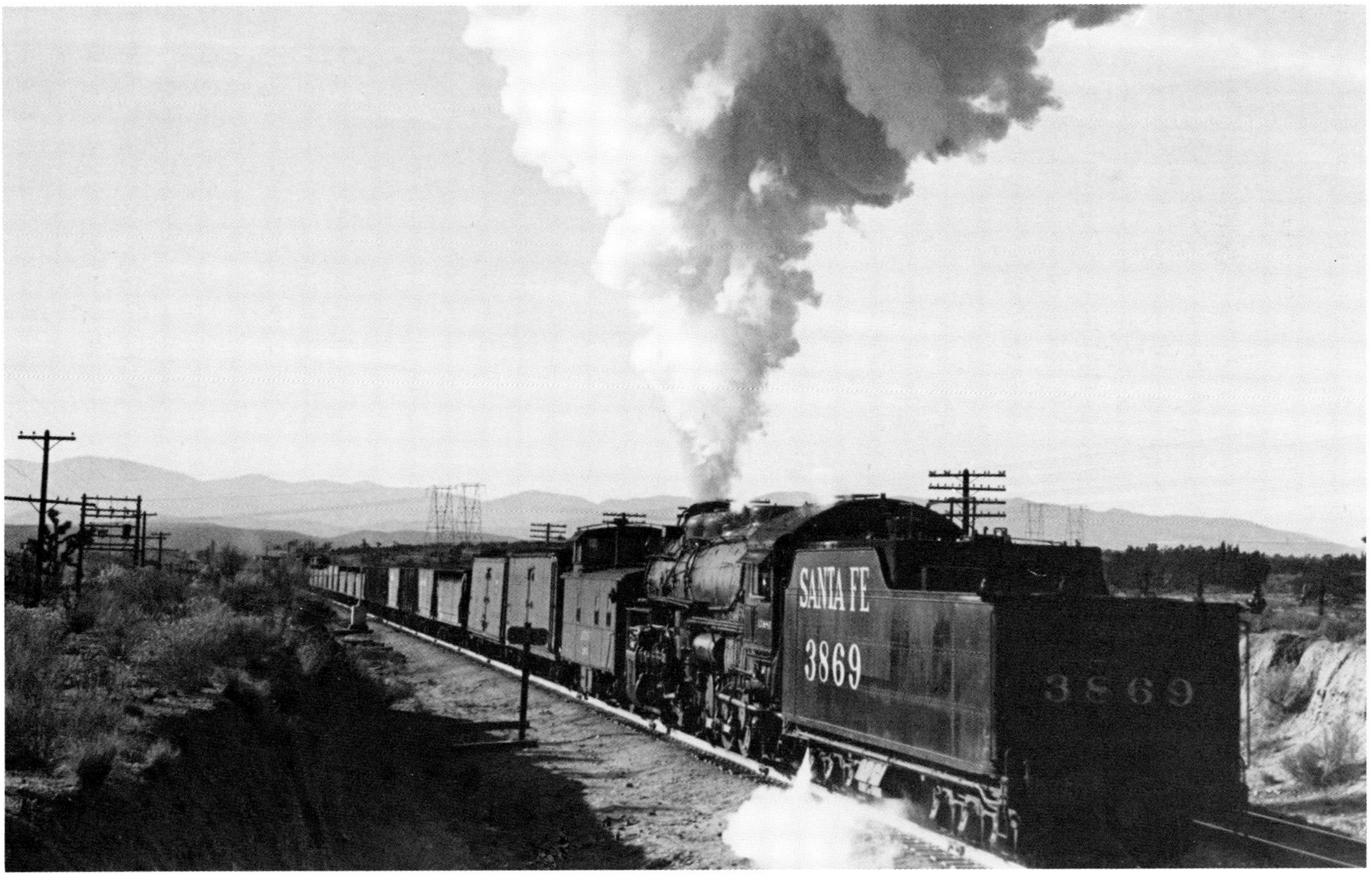
SANTA FE
3869
3869

Top: A doubleheading westbound Union Pacific freight blasts upgrade past the section foreman's house at Hesperia in the late 1930s. The track nearest the camera is the eastward siding. *Fletcher Swan* Above: A westbound Union Pacific freight passing Hesperia in January 1940, with a 5500-class 2-10-2 road engine and 2-8-2 helper 2711 on the point. *Allan Youell*

Top: A westbound Union Pacific passenger train displaying green signals for a following section is seen here between Hesperia and Lugo, circa 1950. The lead unit is a Fairbanks-Morse "Erie-Built," and leads an Alco PA/PB duo. *Thomas Hotchkiss (Author's Collection)* Above left: The depot at Cushenbury and the Pacific Railroad Society special, May 19, 1957. *Chard L. Walker* Above right: A westbound Santa Fe freight pulls into the siding at Hesperia in the 1940s. The head brakeman looks back from his gangway to see when the rear end is in the clear. *Fletcher Swan*

VICTORVILLE ·

Dusk on a winter evening in December of 1964. An 11,000-ton westbound Santa Fe unit coal train has stopped on the main line at Hesperia to allow a westbound passenger to run around it through the siding. The bright spot on the far right is the headlight of the passenger train. *Richard Steinheimer*

Above: This westbound UP Shriners' Special was seen between Hesperia and Lugo on April 28, 1963. *Gordon Glattenberg* Above Right: A 50-50 mix of UP and Rio Grande SD45s lead an eastbound freight toward Thorn on June 19, 1969. The 20-cylinder units are hauling AT&SF freight between Barstow and San Bernardino while their train is being unloaded at the Kaiser Steel mill at Fontana, California. The banner stretched across the long hood of the final D&RGW unit is from the power set's first KAISER COAL run out of the U.S. Steel plant at Geneva, Utah. Bottom Right: Leading three fellow F-units, Santa Fe F7A 283C charges out of Victorville with a westbound train. It's seen here at the west end of the West Victorville siding (Frost) on April 27, 1959. *Two photos: Allan Styffe*

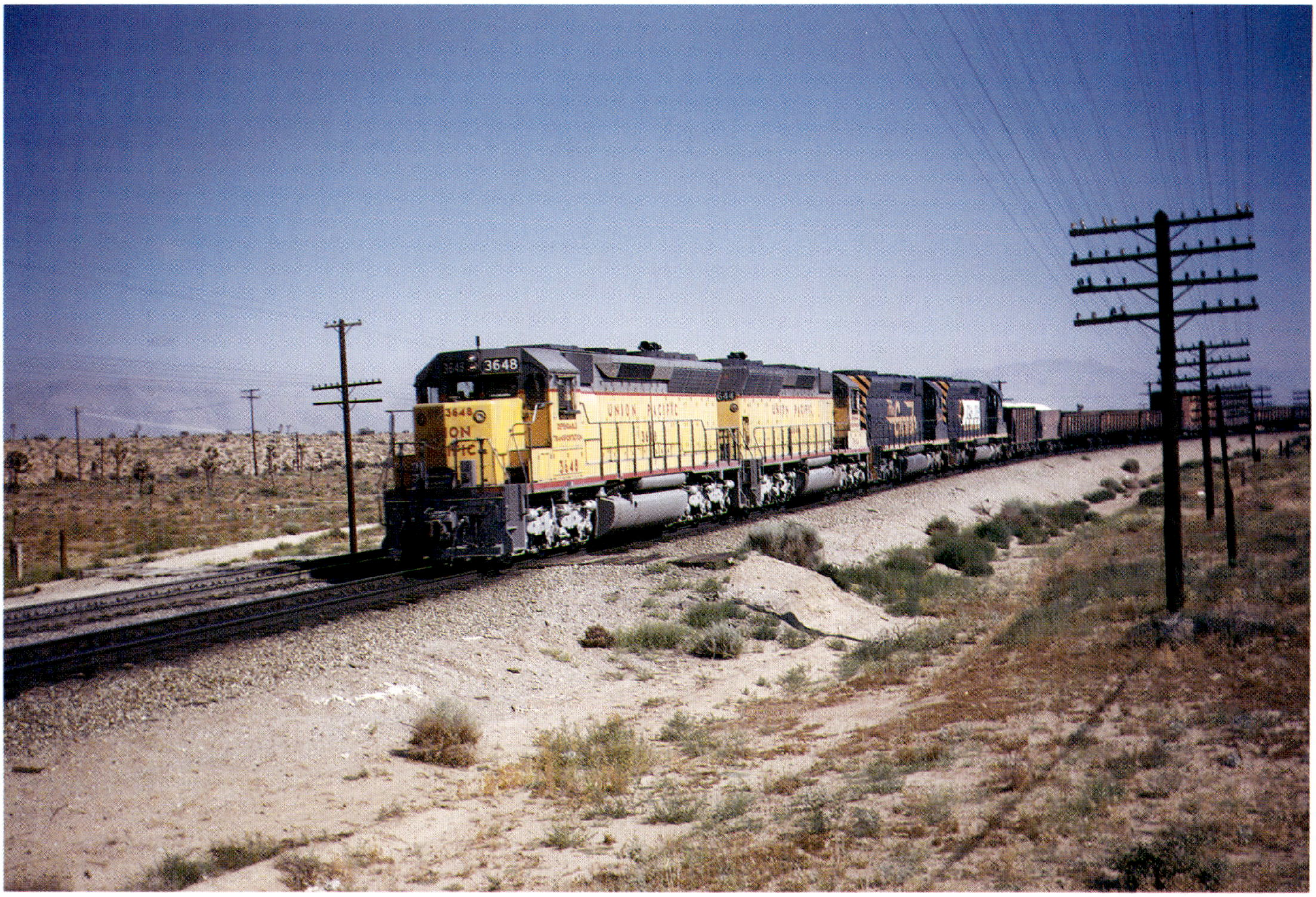
3648
UNION PACIFIC

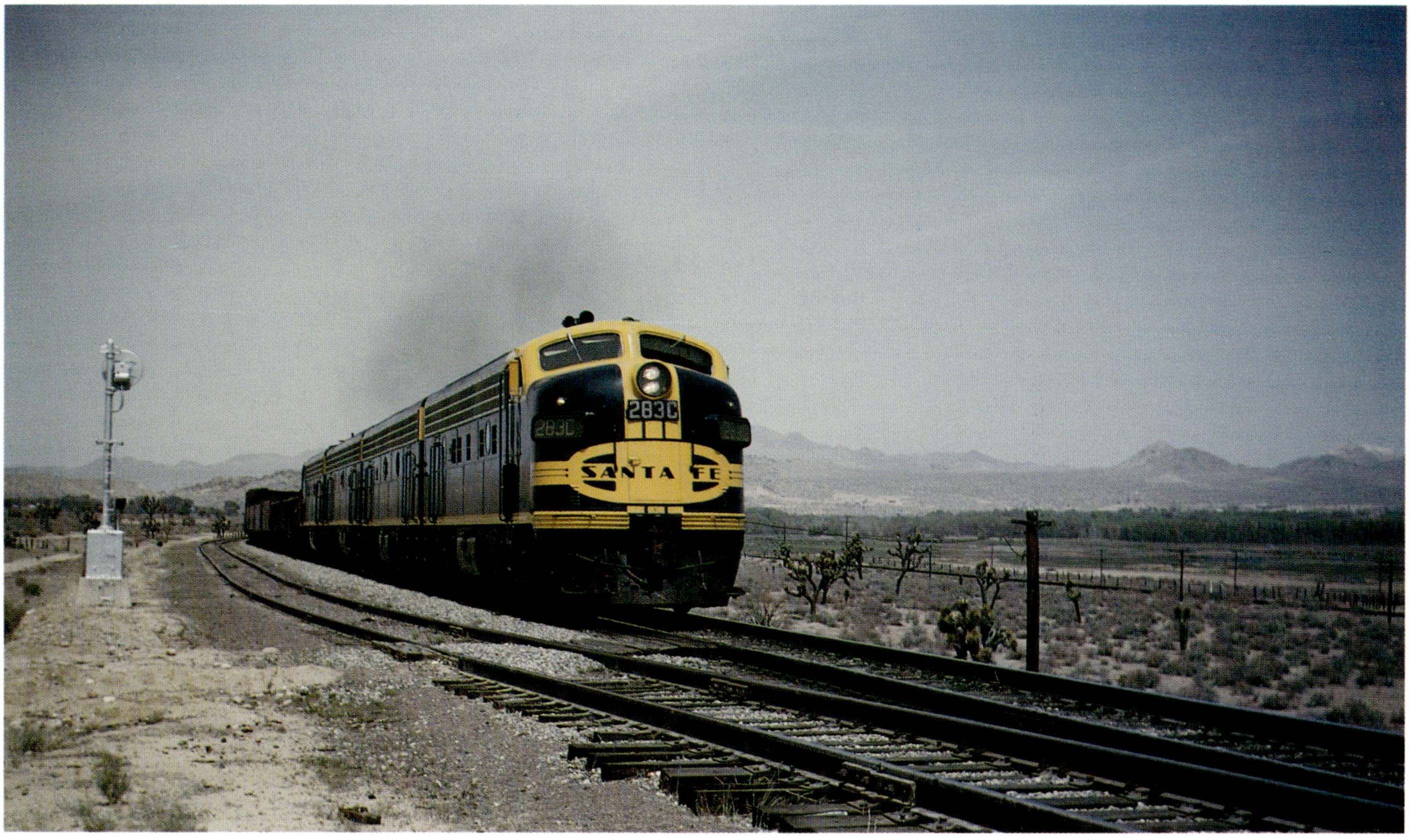
283C
SANTA FE

Top: Santa Fe No. 7, the westbound Fast Mail Express, heads west with Alco PA and PB units between Thorn and Hesperia on March 13, 1954. *Thomas Hotchkiss (Author's Collection)* Above: A pair of 2-10-2s works a westbound AT&SF freight up the grade between Frost and Thorn—where the westward track crosses over the eastward track—around 1950. *Stan Kistler*

Top: AT&SF 4-8-4 2916 brings an overflow section of the westbound GRAND CANYON through Thorn in the early 1950s, with a business car bringing up the markers. *Robert Hale* Above: Propane-fueled Union Pacific gas turbine 57 and its train near Hesperia in December 1953. *James Ady*

On May 4, 1985, the Pacific Railroad Society ran an excursion over Santa Fe's Cushenbury branch, located east of Hesperia. The Amtrak Superliner-equipped train is seen on the return to the AT&SF-UP main lines at Hesperia. *David R. Busse*

Top: Santa Fe train No. 17, the westbound SUPER CHIEF, ascends the grade between Frost and Thorn in the early 1950s. *Richard Steinheimer*
Above: A westbound Shriners' Special, running as Second 23 on June 18, 1950, is doubleheading with 4-6-4 3459 and 4-8-4 2901, seen here near Milepost 39 west of Victorville. *Stan Kistler*

Top: In January 1968, shortly before the Santa Fe discontinued train Nos. 23 and 24—the GRAND CANYON—the train ran with only three cars. In this scene, Alco PAs 58 and 64 are taking No. 23 to Los Angeles. The short train has just crossed over the eastward track between Frost and Thorn. *Chard L. Walker* Above: Union Pacific's LOS ANGELES LIMITED is eastbound at Frost with three Fairbanks-Morse units on March 3, 1951. *Thomas Hotchkiss (Author's Collection)*

A westbound Santa Fe freight with road engine 3844 and helper 3878 (both 2-10-2s) crosses above the eastward track just west of Milepost 39 between Frost and Thorn, and begins its left-hand running to San Bernardino. *Stan Kistler*

Top: A pair of 2-10-2 locomotives leads a westbound freight near West Victorville in 1947, near the eastward track at the far right. *Frank Peterson (Bob Kern Collection)* Above left: Third 23, with 4-8-4 2907, rolls upgrade just above West Victorville in December 1951. A Santa Fe man once remarked, ''No hoghead's gloved hand will ever pull the throttle of a finer engine than a twenty-nine hundred!'' *James Ady* Above right: A westbound Union Pacific at Milepost 40 in the late 1960s. At the left is the east end of the Thorn siding. The ''pot'' signal governed trains in the siding. *Thomas Hotchkiss (Author's Collection)*

Above: In the early 1950s AT&SF No. 23, the westbound GRAND CANYON, crosses over the eastward track near Milepost 39 behind 4-8-4 2915, while in the distance an eastbound disappears through the Upper Narrows. *Robert Hale* Left: In the mid-1970s a westbound Santa Fe freight powered by five SD45s climbs the grade out of Frost. As in the previous photo, a train can be seen just this side of the Upper Narrows in the distance. *Richard Steinheimer*

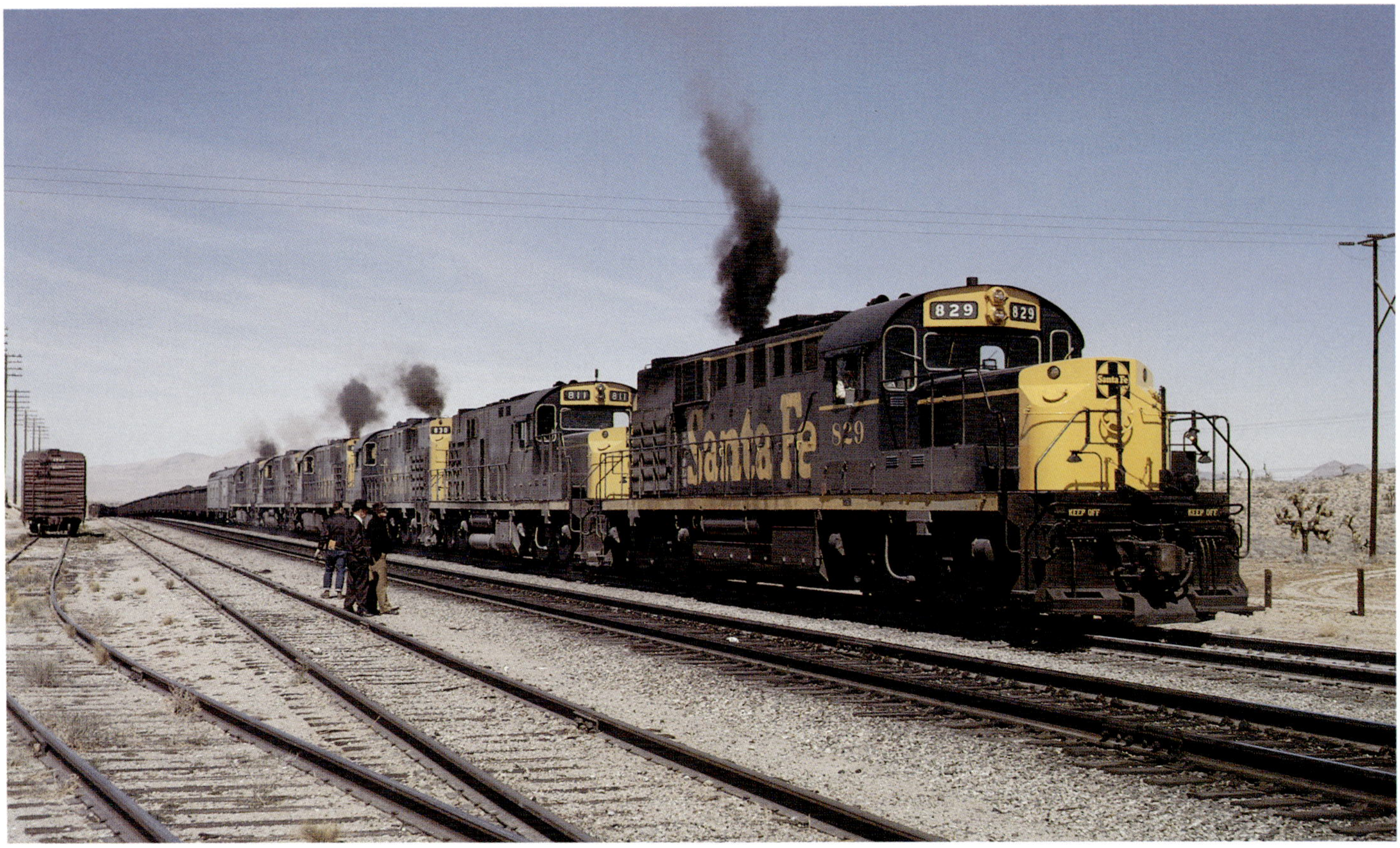
829
Santa Fe
829

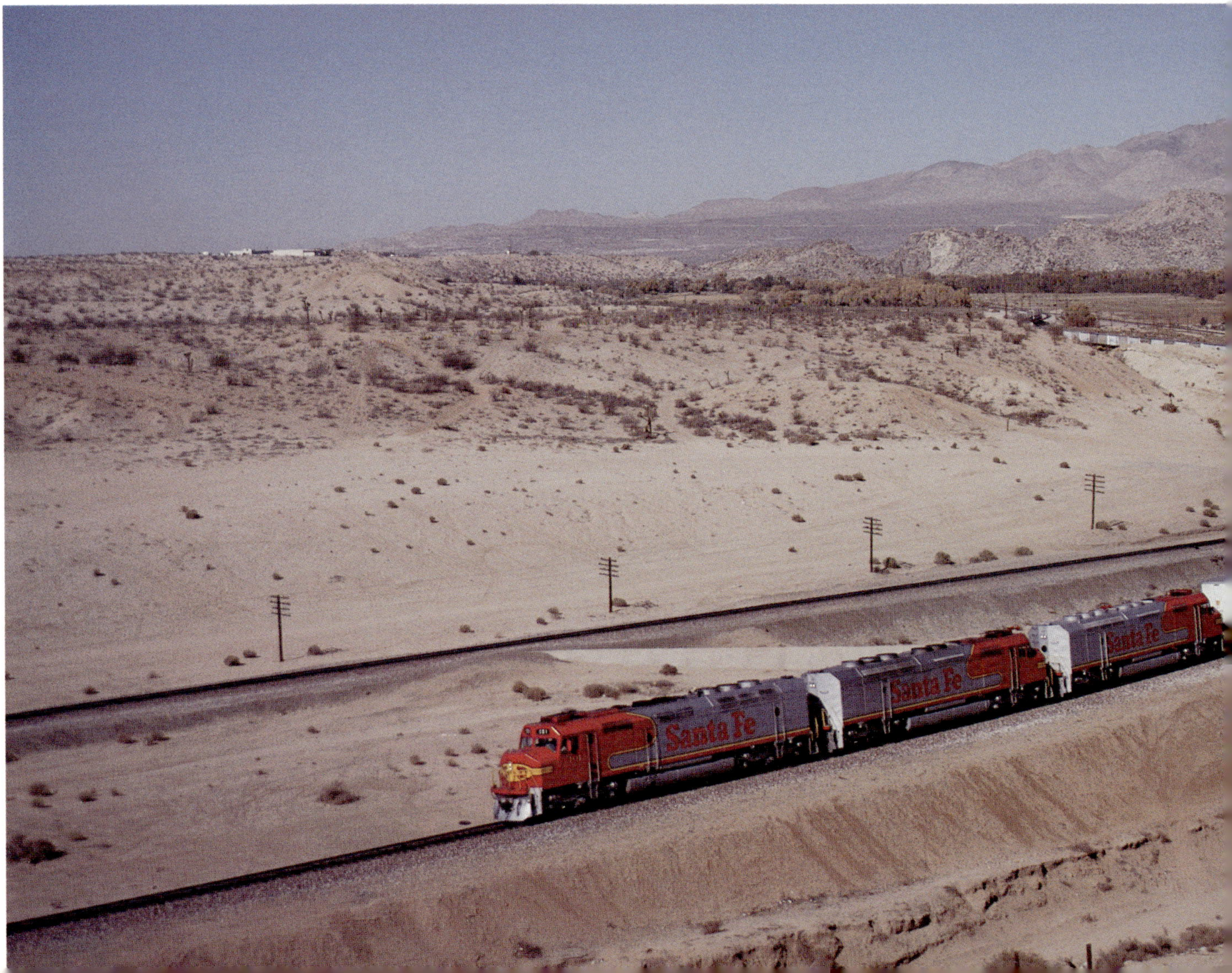
Santa Fe
Santa Fe
Santa Fe

Above Left: Back in 1964 when unit coal trains were still fairly new, this westbound coal drag powered by a quintet of Alco RSD15 "Alligators" is just getting started after replacing a broken knuckle at Thorn. *Chard L. Walker* Above: This view taken in 1985 faces generally north by compass direction, and shows how the former westward track crosses above the former eastward track at mile 39.1 between Thorn and Frost. This flyover was to get trains running right-handed again after operating left-handed from San Bernardino after the line was double-tracked. Left-hand running over Cajon was deemed unavoidable due to the topography in Cajon Canyon. The UP train in the foreground is a westbound, heading for San Bernardino. *David R. Busse* Left: At the same location, three Santa Fe SDFP45s—100, 101, and 102—roll a publicity train of trailers and containers westbound over the flyover on November 16, 1989. The train has just completed an eastbound run through Cajon for company photographers, and is now returning to San Bernardino. Note the rural development in the distant hills of the Mojave Desert—an occurrence which is quickly spreading throughout most of the Victorville/Hesperia area. *Dick Stephenson*

Top: AT&SF 2-10-2 909 brings an eastbound freight through the Upper Narrows back in the 1920s when the railroad was single tracked through the area. This unusual view was taken from atop the large rock formation known as the Gibraltar of the Mojave Desert. The Mojave River is seen at the bottom of the photo. *Bill Hagerman (David Longshore Collection)* Above: A westbound Santa Fe freight with 4-6-2 helper 1325 ahead of 2-10-2 road engine 3886 near West Victorville in July 1946. *Frank Peterson (Bob Kern Collection)*

A westbound Santa Fe 3800-class 2-10-2 road engine and 2-8-2 helper 3130 on the point at West Victorville in 1946. At the right is the rear of an eastbound Union Pacific freight heading for the Upper Narrows. *H.L. Kelso (Author's Collection)*

Above: A westbound Santa Fe freight with F7 units passes through the Upper Narrows in the early 1950s. The rock formation at top center resembles an Indian chief, or George Washington facing upward at a 45-degree angle toward the right. At the moment the photo was taken, a girl happened to be standing on the bridge of his "nose." *Stan Kistler* Opposite top: Number 203 (Union Pacific No. 103, the westbound CITY OF LOS ANGELES, which ran every third day at the time) comes through the Upper Narrows in 1947, while the caboose of an eastbound AT&SF freight passes under the highway bridge. Under the bridge over the Mojave River can be seen the tall stacks of the Southwestern Portland Cement Co. plant at Leon. *Chard L. Walker* Opposite below: The short-lived LAS VEGAS FUN TRAIN that ran for a few weekends the summer of 1976 is seen in the Upper Narrows near Victorville. *Henry Bruekman*

Above: A westbound AT&SF freight with 4-8-2 helper 3739 on the point leaves Victorville in October 1941. At the left is the Victorville Limerock Co. plant. *Ralph Melching* Left: A westbound Union Pacific freight with helper 3555 and road engine 3816 is ready to depart Victorville in October 1945. *Frank Peterson (Bob Kern Collection)* Opposite top: A view of the Victorville depot, circa 1918, when it was on the Mojave River side of the main lines. The depot was later moved across the tracks and placed where this photo was taken from. *Photographer unknown (Charles H. Cox Collection)* Opposite below: Union Pacific train No. 1, the LOS ANGELES LIMITED, leaves Victorville on July 23, 1947, with 4-6-6-4 helper 3817 ahead of -8-4 road engine 839. At the far right a UP helper engine waits on the eastward main to cross over and turn on the wye after the passenger train has departed. *Chard L. Walker*

Above: On a cold morning in November 1948, Santa Fe helper 4027, a 2-8-2, passes the yard limit board just before arriving at Victorville. The track at the left is the siding at West Victorville. *Chard L. Walker* Below: Extra 145 West, powered by a quartet of EMD FT units, passes through the Upper Narrows as it leaves Victorville. The usually dry Mojave River has water in it on this November 19, 1948 morning. *Chard L. Walker*

Top: Union Pacific train No. 104, the CITY OF LOS ANGELES, arrives at Victorville on March 26, 1970, as a typical set of E-unit power pulls alongside the depot. *Allan Styffe* Bottom: On the morning of December 23, 1950, AT&SF train No. 17, the westbound SUPER CHIEF, stopped at Victorville with diesel trouble. Locomotive 3152, the Victorville switcher, was hurriedly placed on the point to help the train to Summit. This view shows them leaving Victorville; the smoke at right in the background is from a UP helper. *Chard L. Walker*

Top: Union Pacific 2-8-2 2710 poses at Victorville in November 1947. This engine was assigned to the Leon Turn for a time. At the left are two pump houses with derricks located over wells, and behind the engine are two large water storage tanks. Also in view is one of the water columns for filling engine tenders. *Jack Whitmeyer* Above: Santa Fe No. 19, the westbound CHIEF, with 4-8-2 road engine 3748 and helper 4-6-2 1346, leaves Victorville on March 25, 1937. A Union Pacific helper waits at left. At the right can be seen two pump houses with derricks, the large vertical water storage tank, and a fuel oil tank. *Francis C. Smith (Stan Kistler Collection)*

Top: A young Chard Walker waves to the fireman on train No. 20, the eastbound CHIEF, as it passes the Victorville depot in the late 1940s. *Richard Steinheimer*

Above: Union Pacific gas-turbine 70 has coupled onto his caboose in the siding at Victorville on July 4, 1962, and is about to pull the train back to set out a bad-order car. First 23, the GRAND CANYON, passes by on the westbound siding, with F3 29 leading five units and 18 cars. *Stan Kistler (Dick Stephenson Collection)*

A classic railroad in a classic desert scene . . . Santa Fe GP35 3403 brings a westbound train through the rocky Lower Narrows between Leon and Oro Grande, as it approaches Victorville in January 1971. *Bob Kern*

Top: A westbound AT&SF freight with three FT units and 2-8-2 helper 3152 on the point waits in the siding at Victorville in the late 1940s. *Fletcher Swan* Above: Mojave Northern Railroad No. 1 works at the Southwestern Portland Cement Co. plant at Leon, just east of Victorville, circa 1950. *Jeff Goodwill*

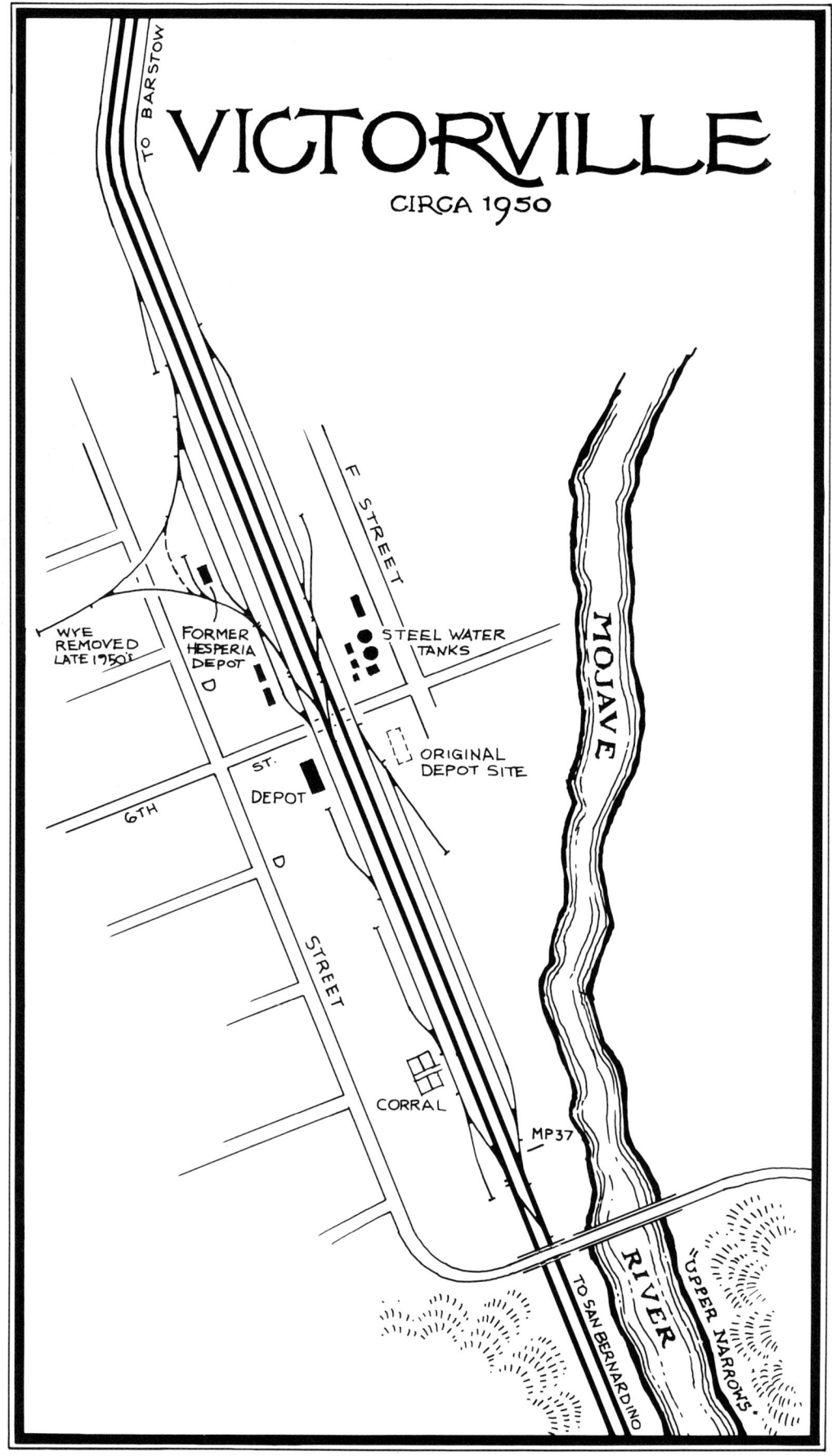

VICTORVILLE

CIRCA 1950

TO BARSTOW

F STREET

MOJAVE

WYE REMOVED LATE 1950's

FORMER HESPERIA DEPOT

STEEL WATER TANKS

ORIGINAL DEPOT SITE

ST. DEPOT

6TH

STREET

CORRAL

MP 37

RIVER

TO SAN BERNARDINO

"UPPER NARROWS"

Above Left: A westbound 198 train with a pair of SDFP45 units in the ''new'' warbonnet scheme passes the signals at East Victorville on July 17, 1989. *Elrond G. Lawrence* Below Left: Extra 2832 West, powered by a long string of four-axle power, passes the Southwestern Portland Cement plant in East Victorville in February 1984. *Bob Kern* Above: An eastbound Union Pacific Super Bowl passenger special passes through the Lower Narrows west of Oro Grande on February 1, 1988, with GP40X units 93 and 95 in charge. *Elrond G. Lawrence*

IN · THE · '80s ·

As shown in the listing on page 172 of *Cajon—Rail Passage to the Pacific,* the very last steam engine to traverse Cajon Pass under its own power for many years was Union Pacific 9000, a three-cylinder 4-12-2 (Union Pacific type) running west as a cab hop on May 3, 1956. It was on its way to the Los Angeles County Fairgrounds in Pomona to be put on display by the Southern California Chapter of the Railway & Locomotive Historical Society.

Just three weeks short of 30 years later, on April 12, 1986, ex-Southern Pacific DAYLIGHT 4449 operated through Cajon Pass on SP's Colton-Palmdale Cutoff, on its way home to Portland, Oregon, after being used in making the Disney movie *Tough Guys* at L.A.'s Taylor Yard and on Kaiser Steel's Eagle Mountain Railroad line near the Salton Sea. This was the first steam engine ever to operate over the cutoff, which was completed in 1967—and resulted in some classic modern images. In the preceding pages, 4449 climbs the grade with its

short passenger train about a mile below Hiland on April 12, 1986. *Leon Callaway* Above, the DAYLIGHT passes through Hiland siding, returning from the *Tough Guys* filming. Just beyond camera range at right is where the old Los Angeles Railway funeral streetcar DESCANSO sat from 1940 until 1967. *Chard L. Walker*

Then, just three years after 4449's run, Union Pacific Northern 8444 (its number until June 1989, when it was returned to its original number of 844) pulled a special passenger train over Cajon on May 5, 1989, en route to Los Angeles for the 50th anniversary of Los Angeles Union Passenger Terminal (LAUPT). The "greyhound" 4-8-4 makes a spectacular sight as it leads its train just west of the Upper Narrows between Victorville and Frost (above right). *Gordon Glattenberg* Less than an hour later, steam power returns to Sullivan's Curve, as 8444 descends the north track on its way to LAUPT (bottom right). *Alan Miller*

Three days later, on May 8, every railfan's dream came true when UP 8444 and SP 4449 steamed their trains up the Cajon Pass grade, side by side from the station of Devore and Dike siding to just west of Summit and Hiland siding. The 4449 had to stop due to a hot bearing alarm, and the 8444 continued on its way east alone.

Needless to say, this great event was witnessed and extremely well documented by not only railfans and the news media, but also by large numbers of non-railfans as well. Fortunately, the weather was nice and clear that day (low clouds, fog, and a light drizzle accompanied the 4449's 1986 run).

May 8, 1989: UP 8444 and SP 4449 pull their respective trains around the big curve just below Blue Cut. *Elrond G. Lawrence* Below, the trains approach Blue Cut with a thunderous show of steam (below left); the 8444 is first to pass the crowds, as it crosses over Blue Cut's stone arch (below center). *Two photos, Leon Callaway* The departing business cars bring up the two trains' markers (below right), along with a final trace of black smoke, in a final Blue Cut view. *Elrond G. Lawrence*

Above: Both trains present a magnificent spectacle in this broadside view just above Blue Cut. *Bill Farmer*
Below: In what has to be the greatest event ever to take place in Cajon Pass, here they come! This view was taken from the hill above Santa Fe's upper tunnel east of Alray. *Joe McMillan*

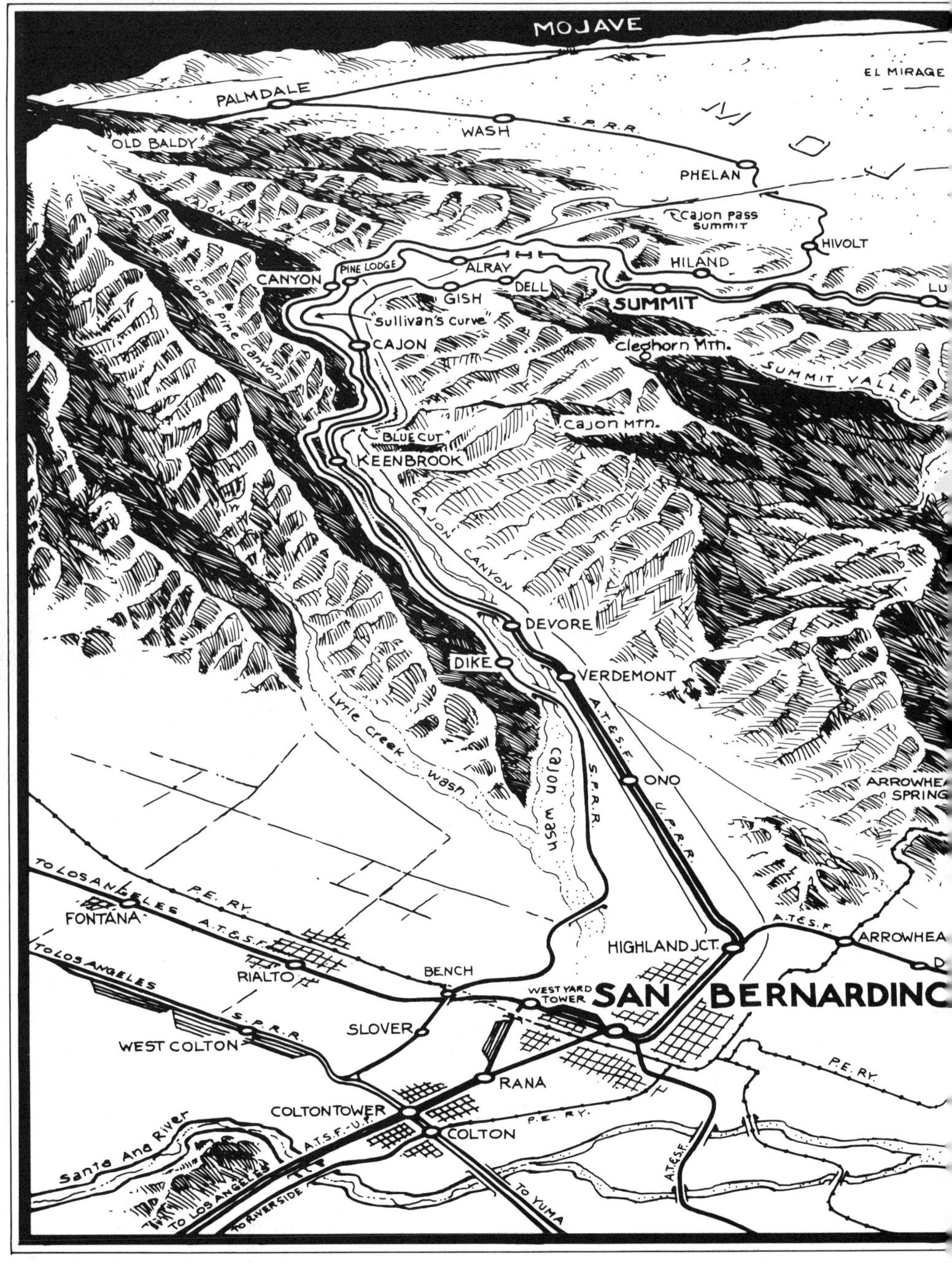